ESTĒE LAUDER ESTĒE LAUDER ESTĒE LAUDER ESTĒE LAUDER ESTĒE LAUDER ESTĒE LAUDER
ESTĒE LAUDER ESTĒE LAUDER ESTĒE LAUDER ESTĒE LAUDER ESTĒE LAUDER ESTĒE LA
ESTĒE LAUDER ESTĒE LAUDER ESTĒE LAUDER ESTĒE LAUDER ESTĒE LAUDER ESTĒE LAUDER
ESTĒE LAUDER ESTĒE LAUDER ESTĒE LAUDER ESTĒE LAUDER ESTĒE LAUDER ESTĒE LA
ESTĒE LAUDER ESTĒE LAUDER ESTĒE LAUDER ESTĒE LAUDER ESTĒE LAUDER ESTĒE LAUDER
ESTĒE LAUDER ESTĒE LAUDER ESTĒE LAUDER ESTĒE LAUDER ESTĒE LAUDER ESTĒE LAUDER
ESTĒE LAUDER ESTĒE LAUDER ESTĒE LAUDER ESTĒE LAUDER ESTĒE LAUDER ESTĒE LA
ESTĒE LAUDER ESTĒE LAUDER ESTĒE LAUDER ESTĒE LAUDER ESTĒE LAUDER ESTĒE LAUDER
ESTĒE LAUDER ESTĒE LAUDER ESTĒE LAUDER ESTĒE LAUDER ESTĒE LAUDER ESTĒE LA
ESTĒE LAUDER ESTĒE LAUDER ESTĒE LAUDER ESTĒE LAUDER ESTĒE LAUDER ESTĒE LAUDER
ESTĒE LAUDER ESTĒE LAUDER ESTĒE LAUDER ESTĒE LAUDER ESTĒE LAUDER ESTĒE LA
ESTĒE LAUDER ESTĒE LAUDER ESTĒE LAUDER ESTĒE LAUDER ESTĒE LAUDER ESTĒE LAUDER
ESTĒE LAUDER ESTĒE LAUDER ESTĒE LAUDER ESTĒE LAUDER ESTĒE LAUDER ESTĒE LA
ESTĒE LAUDER ESTĒE LAUDER ESTĒE LAUDER ESTĒE LAUDER ESTĒE LAUDER ESTĒE LAUDER
ESTĒE LAUDER ESTĒE LAUDER ESTĒE LAUDER ESTĒE LAUDER ESTĒE LAUDER ESTĒE LA
ESTĒE LAUDER ESTĒE LAUDER ESTĒE LAUDER ESTĒE LAUDER ESTĒE LAUDER ESTĒE LAUDER
ESTĒE LAUDER ESTĒE LAUDER ESTĒE LAUDER ESTĒE LAUDER ESTĒE LAUDER ESTĒE LA
ESTĒE LAUDER ESTĒE LAUDER ESTĒE LAUDER ESTĒE LAUDER ESTĒE LAUDER ESTĒE LAUDER
ESTĒE LAUDER ESTĒE LAUDER ESTĒE LAUDER ESTĒE LAUDER ESTĒE LAUDER ESTĒE LA
ESTĒE LAUDER ESTĒE LAUDER ESTĒE LAUDER ESTĒE LAUDER ESTĒE LAUDER ESTĒE LAUDER
ESTĒE LAUDER ESTĒE LAUDER ESTĒE LAUDER ESTĒE LAUDER ESTĒE LAUDER ESTĒE LA
ESTĒE LAUDER ESTĒE LAUDER ESTĒE LAUDER ESTĒE LAUDER ESTĒE LAUDER ESTĒE LAUDER
ESTĒE LAUDER ESTĒE LAUDER ESTĒE LAUDER ESTĒE LAUDER ESTĒE LAUDER ESTĒE LA
ESTĒE LAUDER ESTĒE LAUDER ESTĒE LAUDER ESTĒE LAUDER ESTĒE LAUDER ESTĒE LAUDER
ESTĒE LAUDER ESTĒE LAUDER ESTĒE LAUDER ESTĒE LAUDER ESTĒE LAUDER ESTĒE LA
ESTĒE LAUDER ESTĒE LAUDER ESTĒE LAUDER ESTĒE LAUDER ESTĒE LAUDER ESTĒE LAUDER
ESTĒE LAUDER ESTĒE LAUDER ESTĒE LAUDER ESTĒE LAUDER ESTĒE LAUDER ESTĒE LA
ESTĒE LAUDER ESTĒE LAUDER ESTĒE LAUDER ESTĒE LAUDER ESTĒE LAUDER ESTĒE LAUDER
ESTĒE LAUDER ESTĒE LAUDER ESTĒE LAUDER ESTĒE LAUDER ESTĒE LAUDER ESTĒE LA
ESTĒE LAUDER ESTĒE LAUDER ESTĒE LAUDER ESTĒE LAUDER ESTĒE LAUDER ESTĒE LAUDER
ESTĒE LAUDER ESTĒE LAUDER ESTĒE LAUDER ESTĒE LAUDER ESTĒE LAUDER ESTĒE LA
ESTĒE LAUDER ESTĒE LAUDER ESTĒE LAUDER ESTĒE LAUDER ESTĒE LAUDER ESTĒE LAUDER

ESTĒE

A SUCCESS STORY

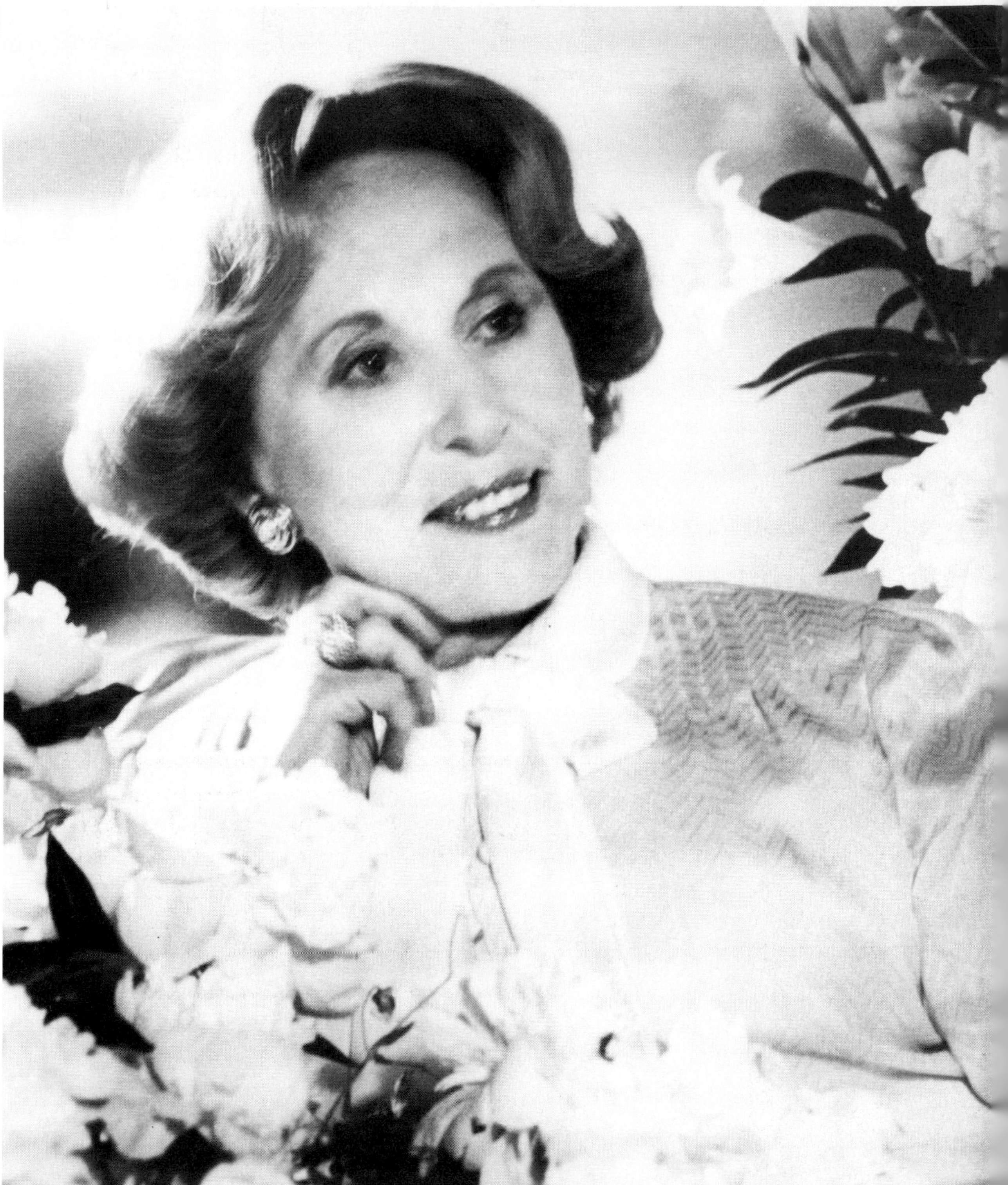
Horst

ESTÉE

A SUCCESS STORY
ESTÉE LAUDER

RANDOM HOUSE
NEW YORK

Library of Congress Cataloging-in-Publication Data
Lauder Estée.
Estée: a success story.
1. Lauder, Estée. 2. Estée Lauder, Inc.—History.
3. Perfumes industry—United States. 4. Cosmetics
industry—United States. 5. Women in business—
United States—Biography. I. Title.
HD9999.P3932L38   1985   338.7′66854 [B]   85–19371
ISBN 0–394–55191–5

TO JOE,

my love, my light, my perfect balance

ACKNOWLEDGMENT

Most especially, I'd like to thank the women of the world who have allowed me to reach out and touch them with beauty.

My family, the sweetest part of my life, has been loving, helpful and patient throughout the preparation of this book.

CONTENTS

PART ONE

DREAMING
THE DREAM

CHAPTER 1

BEGINNINGS

You never realize that you are making a memory at the moment something is actually happening. Stranger still, the strongest memories are those you never dreamed would survive and be inextricably linked to your future. Momentous happenings can lie buried in the past, while tiny, needle-sharp split seconds sometimes stay with you forever. A few haunting notes of a melody, the fragrance of a cherished aunt, a knife-edged encounter—they happen in a moment and they tug at your memory endlessly. They live always, just below your consciousness.

I remember the woman at the Florence Morris Beauty Salon, where I had my first cosmetics concession. She was thoughtless and cruel and will always remain that way in my mind. Maybe she was a catalyst for good in the end; maybe I wouldn't have become Estée Lauder if it hadn't been for her. At the moment she was cast in my memory—to last there *forever*—I despised her. Simply thinking about that incident brings back a twinge of pain.

She was having her hair combed and she was lovely. I was very young and vulnerable, and I loved beauty. I felt I wanted to make contact with her in some small way.

"What a beautiful blouse you're wearing," I complimented her. "It is just so elegant. Do you mind if I ask where you bought it?"

She smiled. "What difference could it possibly make?" she answered, looking straight into my eyes. "You could never afford it."

I walked away, heart pounding, face burning.

Never, never . . . never will anyone say that to me again, I promised myself. Someday I will have whatever I want: jewels, exquisite art, gracious homes—everything.

She's common, I soothed my enraged heart. And she may be pretty, but she has the kind of skin that will look sixty when she's forty.

I could have helped her, but I didn't. I didn't give her a Creme Pack or a sample of my incredible Super-Rich All Purpose Moisturizing Creme. I gave her nothing and, wherever she is, I'm sure her skin looks dreadful.

The woman at the Florence Morris Beauty Salon misused her beauty. Since she was so pretty, she had enormous power to hurt as well as to attract—far more power than if she had been plain.

Beauty has always commanded attention. In a perfect world, we'd all be judged on the sweetness of our souls, but in our less than perfect world, the woman who looks pretty has a distinct advantage and, usually, the last word. Historically, the woman with the smoldering eyes, the sensual mouth, has always been the woman that conquered hearts. Beauty secrets have been passed on from mother to daughter through the ages. Primitive women painted their faces with berry juice. Nero's Roman beauties whitened their faces with chalk. From Cleopatra's fabled milk bath to the ancient Egyptians' pot of black kohl, from the rouged flapper cheeks of the 1920s and the hard, lollipop colors of the Hollywood vamp to Estée Lauder's soft magic, women have always enhanced their God-given looks. It has always been so. It will always be so. A beautiful woman is, well, a beautiful woman. She has always made everyone wish to smile.

Few of us are born with perfect features, which, fortunately, are not needed to radiate beauty. It is care, color, and glow that give the special quality. There are no homely women, only careless women. In all my travels I have never met a woman who couldn't be radiant if she learned how to wield the power of makeup.

An interesting point: beauty is the best incentive to self-respect. You may have great inner resources, but they don't show up as confidence when you don't feel pretty. People are more apt to believe you and like you when you know you look fine. And when the world approves, self-respect is just a little easier. The pursuit of beauty is honorable.

The quintessential woman, the woman who looks lovely as she makes the most of her energy, also has great power if she smells divine. The lingering scent of a beautiful woman as she passes by is one of those memories that unaccountably live forever. Does this sound simplistic? Try smelling divine. You will see that faces become rapt with interest and pleasure. Smelling divine attracts others, gentles their most basic sense, makes them wish to be with you, makes them wish to buy whatever you're selling, whether it's an idea, a product, or a friendship.

One day, when Youth Dew first appeared on the market (what's Youth Dew?—only the most exquisite body fragrance in the world), Millie Considine, who loved to play cards, called me and said, "Can you come over to the '21' Club quickly because we have a game and it's twelve-thirty already?"

I drew a bath, poured in some Youth Dew, bathed quickly, dressed, and dashed outside to hail a taxi.

"Lady, you smell so good," said the driver. "Is that Youth Dew?"

"How in the world do you know?" I asked.

"Well, last week, a lady sat right where you're sitting and I saw her open a bottle and put it on. It was so nice I said I wouldn't charge her for the fare if she gave me the bottle for my wife. She did—it's the best there is. You smell so good I hate to see you leave," continued the driver, "but still, I'm afraid I have to charge you for the fare."

"Of course," I said. "Just keep buying more of that Estée Lauder Youth Dew."

I handed him the fare and a big tip, and couldn't resist a parting line. "By the way, I want you to know I'm Estée Lauder," said I.

"By the way, I want you to know I'm Cary Grant," said he and drove away.

Beauty is a fine invention, if the truth be known. The skilled woman can invent beauty over and over again with extraordinary effect. The art of inventing beauty transcends class, intellect, age, profession, geography—virtually every cultural and economic barrier. There isn't a culture in the world that hasn't powdered, perfumed, and prettied its most adored and fabled women, its most respected women. Love has been planted, wars won, and empires built on beauty. I should know. I'm an authority on all three. Love, wars, and empires have been woven into my personal tapestry for decades. I've been selling Beauty ever since I could recognize Her.

EARLY MEMORIES

The first beauty I ever recognized was my mother, Rose Schotz, a Hungarian beauty whose mother was a French Catholic and whose father was a Hungarian Jew, which accounts, I suppose, for my own ecumenical approach to religion (I belong to both the Catholic Sisters and Temple Emanu-El).

As the story goes, one day my grandmother drew a cup of water from the well and drank it—along with a poisonous spider she hadn't noticed. She died. There was, along with beauty, high drama in my roots. Death by spider—did you ever hear of anything like that in the real world? Upon her demise, my grandfather married again. My mother always missed her own mother and disliked her stepmother. Not surprisingly, she married at fifteen to escape this troubled life.

There the story becomes hazy. My mother seldom spoke of her first marriage, to an older cousin. I know that by the time my mother married my father, she had five sons and a daughter, but I never really knew definitively whether she had been divorced or widowed. I believe she was divorced, which cast a great, black shadow over her life. In those days, it was a disgrace to be divorced. I suppose that's why she was always very vague about the loss or whereabouts of Mr. Rosenthal, her first husband. She used to tell me that when I was happily married, I'd transcend her "burden"—a burden, she'd have been relieved to know, that is shared by one out of two women in America today.

Another fact of which I'm certain is that my mother, who came to my father with six children, was ten years older than he. One can imagine just *how* beautiful she was. In Europe, age rarely seems to be the talked-about factor it is here. Women are admired for their beauty, sensuality, and intelligence, not their youth. In fact, the more "seasoned" a woman is, the more desirable she is. Which brings me to a point I should make immediately. I've vowed to be candid about all in this book, but just don't ask me my age. I've managed to keep that the best-kept secret since D-Day.

I see no reason to alter that stance. Age is an irrelevancy to every woman. *Glow* is the essence of beauty, and it's the absence of radiance that diminishes beauty—at any age. You ask my age? I tell you it simply doesn't matter. I'm fifty, sixty, seventy—whatever you choose. A woman can always have beauty and style. And that is all that matters. Even if age did matter, for the record, I wouldn't tell you.

I've certainly convinced everyone in my family of the unimportance of years. As a matter of fact, a banker with whom we do business was lunching one day with my son Leonard. During the conversation, he asked Leonard his age.

"My age?" answered Leonard. "I'll have to ask my mother. Every time she gives a different interview, I'm a different age. I'll check on what I am this week and let you know."

Still, in my parents' case, the ten-year difference loomed large to my mother. I assume she was especially aware of those years because her first marriage had failed. She was determined to remain lovely and youthful forever for her second husband. I remember an especially poignant moment. I was questioning her about my birth certificate, which gave my father's age as thirty-five to her thirty-eight. She confessed that she had been so sensitive about the age difference that she added seven years to his age when she gave the information to the clerk at my birth. Age was a sensitive issue, no doubt about it. She was always jealous of my father's youth, as well as a bit worried that he might find other women more attractive than she.

"Where are you going?" she'd ask apprehensively as he left the house, a dashing figure in his riding clothes.

An enigmatic response would ensue. "I'll be back in an hour," he'd answer. That's all.

Silence. As soon as he left the house, my mother would begin brushing her hair. She was aware of her responsibility—yes, it is a responsibility—to look as beautiful as she could. I think if every woman made up her face as if her lover or husband were ten years younger than she, we'd be a nation less prone to marital discord. My mother began brushing her golden hair in the morning even before she opened her eyes. I remember her reaching out for that brush as soon as she began to stir, the way business women today reach for their watches. Well, we have two hands, you know: you can reach for the brush with one, and for the watch, with the other.

Mother was very fair, very delicate, and she was never seen outside without her gloves—short, white, crocheted gloves. When the gloves came off, the hands were remarkably smooth and white. Mother said that in Europe when a man kissed a woman's hand, her background showed; hands were as telling as any written pedigree. I would go with her to the pharmacy to buy the largest jar of hand cream in stock, a precaution to ensure she'd never run out of the means to make her hands properly aristocratic just in case a gentleman bent to kiss them.

She wasn't the only one with this idiosyncrasy. One never saw Princess Grace of Monaco without short gloves. Once, the Duchess of Windsor arrived for lunch wearing a pair of tiny lace gloves. When she left, she pulled a pair of white kidskin gloves from her purse. Can you imagine that—two pairs of gloves in one afternoon?

I adored my mother's ornate hairbrush, her hand cream, and the gloves, but the umbrella . . . I despised that umbrella. It was big and black, with an intricately carved silver handle. It never saw rain. My mother would not dream of leaving the house without taking that opened, black umbrella to shield her from the sun. I would wither with embarrassment. Always, when the umbrella was opened, I walked several steps behind her, dreading being seen with her on a sparkling summer afternoon under a huge, dark parasol.

"Mama . . . it is just too eccentric . . ." I would complain to no avail. My mother knew that the sun was terrible for skin years before modern scientists and dermatologists told it to the world. That hated parasol would always accompany her in the summertime, notwithstanding my mortification, and my mother's skin remained soft and supple until the day she died.

When she did die, at eighty-eight, she was still beautiful and still certain of her appeal.

"You're as beautiful as you think you are," she'd tell me. She walked tall when she entered a room and held her head triumphantly. "The secret," she'd whisper, "is to imagine yourself the most important person in that room, the person everyone else is waiting to see. If you imagine it vividly enough, you will become that person."

Her style was remarkable. Her style was an art form. She was discreet, elegant, and deeply committed to family, particularly my father.

He was Max Mentzer, a Czechoslovakian horseman, an elegant, dapper monarchist in Europe, who, when transported to a new country, still carried a cane and gloves on Sundays. When he was not attending to business or out riding, he was buying land, a penchant I have inherited—the land buying, that is, not the serious horseback riding. The difference between us is that he was satisfied with just the acreage, whereas I have always liked to have airy, comfortable homes on my land.

When my father was a young man, Emperor Franz Joseph wanted his niece, who weighed about 300 pounds, to marry him, but somehow Father got out of that. He was waiting for Rose. Waiting, perfectionist that he was, for his ideal even though he had to elude the Emperor's niece in the process. Along with his love for acquiring land, I also inherited his genes for high standards—things must be perfect to be acceptable. By perfect, I don't mean expensive, necessarily, or vast or rare. I mean, well, perfect. As in the perfect phrase, the perfect gift.

The gracious Lillian Carter, the mother of the ex-President, understood this. Once, when Jimmy Carter was President, Miss Lillian came to New York. My husband was asked to escort her to a charity function. Joe was so taken by her candor and charm, he asked me to give a luncheon in her honor, which I did. Joe was right. She was unique. She spoke happily about her son, the President (we all felt that had a nice ring to it). I'm not sure whether Mr. Carter took her advice regularly, but after hearing her at the luncheon, I'm certain it was tendered. A few days later, the postman delivered an extravagant box of . . . hominy grits. It was the one thing she was sure I didn't have—and the perfect gift. Now, I *do* admire perfection, as did my father.

I was not born in Germany, Czechoslovakia, Austria, or Hungary. I have read that I was born in all of these romantic places in various published accounts, but I was actually born at home, in the style of the time, at 9 Hillside Avenue in Corona, New York, on a quiet street in the borough of Queens. My mother named me Esty, after her favorite Hungarian aunt. Complicating the picture was an Italian wet nurse, who encouraged my mother to name me Josephine, Josephine being her favorite Milanese aunt. My mother concurred, partly out of gratitude for the wet nurse's services, partly because, I suspect, she considered Josephine a true American name.

The plot thickens. When the time for birth certificate registration rolled around, no official clerk had ever heard of Esty, let alone knew how to spell it, but Esther they knew, so Josephine Esther Mentzer became my official name. It was to change yet again when my father registered me in school.

"Her name is Esty," he told the principal.

Esty? Again, there was a spelling problem. My father's English was not up to it.

Josephine Estée Mentzer became the school version from then on, for it certainly sounded like Estée when my father said Esty.

The accent? I believe it came from an enterprising teacher who took it upon herself to add a little romantic French touch to the Hungarian-Czechoslovakian-Milanese name in her roll book.

To my family, none of those niceties prevailed. I was Esty to them and still am.

I might mention, right here, that I've never talked about my personal life so openly before. It has always been my feeling, especially when my children and grandchildren were young, that public personalities should be reserved about their private lives. One's family, after all, has not asked to be spotlighted in a very public glare. All these years I have guarded my privacy because I believed that what I achieved in public was the public's right to know, but what mattered in our home was ours and ours alone. With this book, all that changes. I've read so many myths about myself that it's time to set the record straight.

PLANTING PASSIONS

I was the cherished, rather fragile, coddled baby of the family. My very first memory is of my mother's scent, her aura of freshness, the perfume of her presence. My first sensation of joy was being allowed to reach up and touch her fragrant and satiny skin. Her hair didn't escape my attention, either. As soon as I was old enough to hold a brush, I'd give her no peace.

"Esty, you've already brushed my hair three times today," I can still hear her complaining gently. My older sister, Renee, submitted to getting her face patted with my mother's cream when she'd rather have been left alone to read or paint. Only my beautiful sister-in-law Fanny was perpetually saintlike in her submission to my "treatments." She'd endure my brushing her long hair for what must have seemed like eons as I stood on a kitchen chair to reach her head.

All of this annoyed my father considerably. "Stop fiddling with other people's faces," he'd say.

But that is what I liked to do—touch other people's faces, no matter who they were, touch them and make them pretty. Before I'm finished, I'll set, I'm certain, the world's record for face touching . . . and I'm nowhere near finished, I might add.

I could spin magic on the faces of my family. As soon as school was over, I'd run home, feed a lump of sugar to my horse, Bessie, then start on faces and hair. Pretty clothes were another passion, one that has not yet left me and, at this stage, is not likely to. I recall a knitted hat that a friend of my mother's made for me. I was distinctly ungrateful because it was so plain. I asked her to add two pom-poms, one on either side of the hat. Nothing else would do. Even though the words "high fashion" had not yet entered my vocabulary, even though Givenchy was still in knee pants himself, I just knew instinctively that pom-poms would make that hat high fashion. Even at eight, being fashionable, being feminine, being different, was a *raison d'être* for me. And I was right. My teacher paraded me before another, older, class to my immense satisfaction, and I displayed, with appropriate grandeur, my beautiful pom-pommery. Even then I knew.

I loved the touch of beautiful fabrics. One of my half brothers, my mother's son by her first marriage, was much older than I. He, in partnership with another man, opened a large dry-goods store in Corona. The store, with its unfanciful name—Plafker and Rosenthal—was my gateway to fancy. It was Dress-Up Land for me. I loved to play with the beautiful clothes, touch the smooth, leather gloves, pull the lace scarves around my shoulders. Fanny, my half brother's wife, smiled indulgently at my imagination.

My father was a man of many professions. When he first came to America, leaving behind privileged life, he brought with him valises filled with dapper clothes . . . and no profession that was meaningful on these shores. First, he looked for work in the neighborhood. Having little knowledge of English and fewer skills, he met with problems. One day, he walked into a neighborhood tailor shop in search of cuffs. The tailor, who admired my father's aristocratic bearing, offered him work . . . as a custom tailor. Willing to try, my father soon discovered that he didn't have the hands for the needles.

Eventually, he bought a hardware store on Corona Avenue with savings he had brought from Europe. He supplied the local builders with fixtures and appliances, and they, in turn, supplied him with real estate tips. One of his earliest interests, in fact, was a New Jersey cemetery. Throughout my entire childhood the cemetery was a place to play, since it was full of trees and flowers and absolutely empty of bodies. Years later, the greatest excitement for my own children was a Sunday excursion to "Poppa's cemetery." My father kept his horses and a wonderful sulky on the grounds, which included a well-laid-out trotting track. Each boy would be allowed to take a fast trot before we all settled down to a picnic. Picnics and ponies at the cemetery—it was an idyllic time! If you were to fly over the same cemetery today, you'd see its main roadway is the same oval track my father's ponies trotted.

My father's hardware store was my own first venture into merchandising. I loved to help him arrange his wares. My special job was creating window displays that would attract customers. How I loved to make those windows appealing! I would have been a superb window dresser today, when the work is an art form, but then, I had to be satisfied with placing the giftware under an artificial Christmas tree or showing off our gift wrapping by covering a hammer or a set of nails with extravagant bows and papers, which really did seem to delight his customers. Packaging required special thought. You could make a thing wonderful by its outward appearance. Little did I think I'd be doing the same thing, multiplied a billionfold, in not too many years. There may be a big difference between lipstick and dry goods, between fragrance and doorknobs, but just about everything has to be sold aggressively. I honed my techniques as I played with the wares at my father's store and at Plafker and Rosenthal. I whetted my appetite for the merry ring of a cash register. I learned early that being a perfectionist and providing quality was the only way to do business. The ladies in their furs came to buy, and smiled and bought more when I waited on them. I knew it. I felt it.

I found *my* first fur on a floor. My mother and I were visiting a wealthy cousin in the movie industry. I was fascinated by the leopard skin reposing nobly, face frozen in a perpetual scowl, under my cousin's coffee table. While the grown-ups chatted in one room, I yielded to temptation and wrapped myself in that rug. I walked to and fro with great majesty, I recall. Much to my embarrassment, I was caught in the act. My very generous and amused cousin presented me with the trophy. Mother, rug, and I went off to the furrier, who transformed the leopard skin into a leather-trimmed coat. To this day, I still have it.

Rapture, I learned early, is wearing exotica. Today, of course, I take care that the exotica is not an endangered species. Rapture, I knew then and know even more strongly now, is feeling pretty—and very special.

I want to paint a picture of the young girl I was—a girl caught up, mesmerized by pretty things and pretty people. Thinking about my childhood now reveals such early patterns. My drive and persistence were always there, and those are qualities that are essential for building a successful business. Still, I sometimes wonder if I had set my heart on selling tassels, cars, furniture, or anything else but beauty, would I have risen to the top of a profession? Somehow I doubt it. I believed in my product. I loved my product. I loved to touch the creams, smell them, look at them, carry them with me. A person has to love her harvest if she's to expect others to love it. And beauty was such a bountiful harvest.

How can I have known this at twelve? I don't understand it—I just did. That's why I wrapped myself in the leopard rug, why I had no choice but to wrap myself in that sumptuous fur. It was so colorful I couldn't resist.

All was not idyllic in my childhood, but when trouble struck, my sister, not I, absorbed the blow.

One year, the specter of an infantile paralysis epidemic loomed over New York. My mother, terrified, fled with my sister and me to relatives in Milwaukee, Wisconsin. We stayed for months and months—a happy time for me. It was *so* happy that, years later, I always felt and still do that I'd put down roots there, that it was, indeed, another home. My father, according to plan, would write us when the danger passed and we could safely return. And so he did. We left Wisconsin and returned home, but prematurely as it happened. My sister, to our horror, contracted polio; I somehow was spared. We all rallied around Renee, who wore a brace till she was fifteen. She was plucky and kind spirited throughout her ordeal, and she set many standards of bravery and endurance for all of us.

In those days, as now, beauty and health were very much intertwined. My mother took the "baths" religiously. They were good for her skin, good as a purge to draw out impurities from the system, and good as a social ground to talk and gossip with the other women. First she'd go to spas in Europe, to Carlsbad, Czechoslovakia, or Baden-Baden, Germany. Later she'd take me along when she went to Saratoga Springs in upstate New York. I was vastly impressed. Steaming vapors. Plush terrycloth towels. Face creams that smelled like heaven. My mother's cream, in particular, was divine. It was The Formula, she told me; something from Europe. A mystery. I watched her apply the cream to her face, then remove the excess with the back of her hand so not a drop would be wasted and her hands would benefit. Those were sweet days. She had only two or three simple dark dresses, but they were always the sheerest of silks, the most gossamer of textures. My mother was always gazed upon with admiration at health spas.

At home, in America, her accent tended to isolate us. She spoke a very broken English, with a predominantly German accent, and we were at war with Germany during my childhood. Those foreign sounds fell on the unfriendly ears of those who had loved ones in the war— and that was almost everyone. My mother seemed so old to me. And so old-fashioned.

I tried to discourage her from coming to school to speak with my teachers and other parents. I remember one friend's mother reading fairy tales to us in her dulcet American tones. My mother wasn't able to read anything to me. In fact, although my father spoke more English, both were European in every straightlaced way—and I wanted desperately to be 100 percent American.

So I was torn. I loved them both so much—their beauty and their character, but I didn't love feeling different because of their old-country ways. I always seemed to be an apologist for them. On reflection, it seems that children strive to be like one another, while adults are always searching for the unusual, the different. At least, this adult does. When I was young, I shunned my European background. Today, I derive huge pleasure from the friends I've made who allow me glimpses into lives I've never led. One of the dearest of those friends is the royally beautiful Begum Aga Khan, who was Miss France in her youth and who stands six feet tall in her indescribably exquisite saris. She's my neighbor and friend in the south of France and the widow of Aga Khan III (the grandfather of the present Aga Khan) and step-grandmother of Princess Yasmin Aga Khan, Rita Hayworth's daughter.

The Begum, as you can imagine, has a story very different from mine, and yet our communication is perfect—*perfect*. In fact, her advice quite literally saved my life once, about which I'll tell you later. When I was young, though, I would not have been impressed by the European beauty. I was caught up with American glamour. When I dreamed, in my private universe, I dreamed of being a skin specialist and making women beautiful, since I had heard that many in my mother's family did just that.

When I was feeling romantic, I dreamed of being an actress—name in lights, flowers, handsome men. Actresses were the epitome of beauty and glamour. My father considered my desire to be an actress even more alarming than my penchant for making others beautiful. Sometimes, I dreamed of being married. *That* was acceptable to him.

One thing I promised myself: if I ever did get married, I would live in Manhattan. My excursions to that extraordinary place filled me with solemn joy. I was awed by the stores overflowing with treasures and by the fashionable women with their princess walks and their lustrous furs. It was entrancing. I knew someday I would be a part of it all. But at the time, I had to be content with brushing Fanny's hair. It was enough to occupy me for a while, but not for long . . .

In every life there is a moment—an event or a realization—that changes that life irrevocably. If the change is to be a happy one, one must be able to recognize the moment and seize it without delay. Rose Kennedy once told me that good luck is something you make and bad luck is something you endure, a very wise observation indeed. People do make their luck by daring to follow their instincts, taking risks, and embracing every possibility.

SEIZING THE MOMENTS

My shining moment came in the form of a quiet, bespectacled man who also loved touching faces.

Uncle John Schotz. Charming, erudite, inquiring, my mother's brother came to visit us from Hungary. He was a skin specialist. What glories those words conjured up!

On the heels of Uncle John's arrival came a terrible war in Europe. I was too young to understand its implications, but I did understand that because of its horrors, Uncle John had to stay in America. Secretly, I rejoiced.

He captured my imagination and interest as no one else ever had. I was smitten with Uncle John. He understood me. What's more, he produced miracles. I watched as he created a secret formula, a magic cream potion with which he filled vials and jars and flagons and any other handy container. It was a precious velvety cream, this potion, one that magically made you sweetly scented, made your face feel like spun silk, made any passing imperfection be gone by evening. Maybe I'm glorifying my memories, but I believe today that I recognized in my Uncle John my true path. He produced his glorious cream in our home, working happily over a gas stove, mixing in first one ingredient, which he seemed to conjure up out of nowhere, then another, then another. I watched and learned, hypnotized. He mixed and stirred—as passionate as any alchemist—until the ingredients were transformed into cream. Snow cream.

He was aghast when I washed my face with soap. "Soap on the face? No! No soap, Estée darling, please. Soap is made with the harshest of detergents that dry." But the gentle oil that he used in his cream was good. It cleansed, lubricated, and protected. Oil, he explained, could cut through the residue of the day as well as cleanse excess body oils that tended to clog pores.

Oil to do away with oil? It was a mystery to me. Uncle John explained. "It takes oil to cut oil. When you have an oily stain on your dress, you can remove it with another oil, like turpentine. Neither water nor soap will be effective. A gentle, very thin layer of oil on the skin nourishes and protects—and it cuts through the thicker oil exuded by the pores."

I loved to hear the language—it seemed to me a marvelous code— "cleanse," "freshen," "nourish," . . .

If I had to use water on my face, said Uncle John, I was to apply a thin layer of his oil-rich cream over my still damp skin to lock in the moisture. My education was just starting, but first, I was to discard that detergent soap, the only soap available in those years.

"Listen to me, Estée," said Uncle John. "Just try my cream." *Try* it? I was devoted to it. I loved his creams, loved his potions, loved my Uncle John, who was going to stay in America—near me. In fact, he eventually opened his own, small office for his European clientele in Manhattan.

This is the story of a bewitchment. I was irrevocably bewitched by the power to create beauty.

Uncle John had worlds to teach me.

We constructed a laboratory of sorts in the tiny stable behind the house. My parents installed gleaming linoleum on the floors and walls. We set up a table, where I watched my uncle mix his magic.

Do you know what it means for a young girl to suddenly have someone take her dreams quite seriously? Teach her secrets?

I could think of nothing else. After school, I'd run home to practice being a scientist. I began to value myself so much more, trust my instincts, trust my uniqueness. With my uncle I was preoccupied with research into possibilities—mine. Trusting oneself does not always come naturally. If learned when young, the practice sticks. Today, there is no one who can intimidate me because of title or skill or fame. I do what's right for *me*. Recently, a well-known decorator, who shall be nameless here, found this out. While we were walking up the winding staircase of my home in New York, she said to me, with a sweep of her hand that encompassed everything I'd decorated, "I could do wonders with this."

I patted her sagging cheeks. My confidence had been born years before. "I could do wonders with these," I said.

If I was to be a scientist with Uncle John, I needed live subjects on whom to experiment. I didn't have a single friend who wasn't slathered in our creams. If someone had a slight redness just under her nose that was sure to emerge into a sensitive blemish the next day, she'd come to visit. I'd treat her to a Creme Pack—*voilà!*—vastly improved skin the next day. Friends of friends of friends appeared. I devised a name for my uncle's cream—Super-Rich All Purpose Creme. My reputation among my peers at Newtown High School grew by leaps and bounds. I gave away gallons of cream to friends!

Deep inside, I knew I had found something that mattered much more than popularity. My moment had come and I was not about to miss seizing it. Uncle John loved me, I loved him, and my future was being written in a jar of snow cream.

Another pivotal moment was looming on the horizon, one that would also change my life irrevocably. I did not recognize this opportunity quite as quickly as I grasped Uncle John's magic.

It came in the form of a brash young man in knickers. Tall and handsome, he carried golf clubs, walked with a jaunty, sure step, and had a smile that made my heart dissolve. Naturally, I ignored him. I'll tell you why.

I was very young. We did not talk about boys, let alone date them. My father would have been very disappointed in me if I had had young men on my mind. Virtue and morality and lofty thought were expected to emanate from me like an unbroken stream of moonlight.

My father was more lenient with my sister, Renee. She was a few years older and still limping from her bout with polio. Father was persuaded to allow her to rent a tiny bungalow in Mohegan Lake, New York, with friends. She needed fun, and rules were bent for her.

It was wonderful at the lake, wrote Renee. "Do send Estée for a few days. We'll all take care of her, every moment. We promise!"

I was delirious with joy when my parents agreed. They put me on a train, to be met by Renee at the other end. Two blissful days of sun and swimming followed. On the third day, my parents followed, just to make certain we were all right.

Then the tragedy occurred. Another young girl went swimming, caught her head under the long wooden pier, and drowned. The terrible accident galvanized my parents into swift action. They gathered up both of us, ignoring our protestations, and immediately left for home.

Hell hath no fury like a young woman spirited away from a place she loves. I didn't let my parents rest. Just a day or so later, we took a drive and saw a tiny bungalow with a "For Sale" sign opposite the Rock Hill Lodge Country Club in Mohegan Lake. My father gave the owner a check on the spot. It seemed a small price for family peace. The house had one tiny bedroom, with a brass bed; a kitchen, with one table, several chairs, and a fold-out cot; an outhouse. It was heaven. Eventually my parents built a larger house on the property. The new house had a big open porch and a wonderful, old-fashioned swing. It was on this porch, one day, during the hottest summer anyone could remember, that I was swinging back and forth when my future strolled by.

Tennis was the rage. That morning, I was hoping a threesome who needed a fourth might happen by. Since it was so hot, I was almost sure that if I sat there long enough on my porch, I'd find a game.

I was wearing a pink blouse, striped bloomers, and socks.

He, as I said, was splendid in knickers. He was on his way to the Rock Hill Lodge for the weekend.

"Hello, Blondie!" he called out to the bloomer girl on the swing.

I froze.

I remember blushing furiously, my face and neck getting hot with embarrassment. "Hello, Blondie" would *not* have pleased my father. I did not answer, just turned away, and thought about him every moment all the next week.

The next weekend, a friend of my sister's visited us. "There's a young man at the club who would like to be introduced to you," he told me. "Properly introduced." He winked. "A Mr. Joseph Lauter. He's nice. Really. He told me to tell you so."

That was a different story. I was relieved. Mother and Father said yes to a proper introduction. He turned out to be sweet and surprisingly shy for such a bold "Hello, Blondie." He was the most gentle person. I had my first beau.

He apologized for calling me Blondie, then invited me for a canoe ride.

That was the beginning. He was an older man . . . not really, but older than I. My mother approved of the age difference. She adored Joseph, and so did I. All at once I felt noticed, cherished, grown-up, amused, amusing, happy. We went on many romantic canoe rides and countless long walks. After a time, we were betrothed. What a wonderful word—"betrothed"—so much more elegant than "engaged." Love interfered, it really did, and postponed my dreams of being a skin specialist (and certainly an actress). But one dream looked promising. True love managed to find me a husband who felt as I did about Manhattan. Joseph promised me we would live there as soon as we were married. We talked about Joe's name—Lauter. Originally, in Austria where Joe's father was born, the family name was Lauder. When Joe's father came to America, an immigration officer heard the *d* as a *t* and in the new country, Lauder became Lauter. Joe and I decided that we would return his name to the integrity of the original so that the family we hoped to create would honor his father's proper heritage. Little did either of us dream it would become a worldwide symbol of beauty.

My wedding picture was in the rotogravure section of the New York *Times*. Somehow, after all these years of so many newspaper pictures, that one still ranks as the greatest thrill. I wore an off-white satin gown cut in a princess style with a V neckline. It was fashionably short in front and long in back. On my head I wore a delicate cap, to which was attached the world's longest train. In my arms I carried calla lilies. For the first time in her life, the future cosmetics queen wore lipstick. Her father made her take most of it off.

Handsome men crossed canes high over our heads as we walked down the aisle, Joe and I. I loved my wedding.

Josephine Estée Mentzer became Josephine Estée Lauder.

The bride's skin was glowing. Naturally. Estée Lauder was about to be born.

CHAPTER 2

TELEPHONE, TELEGRAPH, TELL-A-WOMAN

When I first met her, Helena Rubinstein looked like a Russian tsarina, with ruby rings the size of birds' eggs on her fluttering fingers, but the skin of her neck was less than perfect. Elsa Maxwell had introduced us at the April in Paris Ball. I was young, very eager, and still new in my career . . . also a trifle inexperienced in dealing with tsarinas. I declared that I was pleased to meet her, that her face looked absolutely lovely but my Creme Pack could do wonders for her neck. She looked at me hard, very hard, then asked me to send it. Helena Rubinstein was not one to let anything escape her.

Terribly embarrassed the next day at realizing how rude I must have sounded, I sent off the Creme Pack. My motives were pure, they truly were; I wanted to help. I believed then, as I do now with even more intensity, that the proper cream can provide a face-lift effect and can increase blood circulation without the harmful effects of manipulation. But, I'm getting ahead of myself. Helena Rubinstein in the earliest years was as far removed from me as the Duke of Windsor.

We were struggling so hard to be independent, Joe and I, and sometimes this was not easy. Times were lean. About two years after our marriage, we had a beautiful son, and I spent my days mothering Leonard. And all the time, all the time, I was also mothering my zeal for experimenting with my uncle's creams, improving on them, adding to them. I was forever experimenting on myself and on anyone else who came within range. Good was not good enough—I could always make it better. I know now that "obsession" is the word for my zeal. I was obsessed with clear glowing skin, shining eyes, beautiful mouths. It was never quiet in the house. There was always a great audible sense of industry, especially in the kitchen, where I cooked for my family and during every possible spare moment, cooked up little pots of cream for faces. I always felt most alive when I was dabbling in the practice cream. I felt as though I was conducting a secret, absorbing experiment—a real adventure . . .

THE PLAY'S THE THING—FOR NOW

I continued to love dressing up. When Leonard was very young, I searched for ways to put all my loves together. It was simply not enough for me to stay home and play Mommy. I was yearning for bright lights. I'd wander down to the Cherry Lane Theater and ask them to give me small parts in their productions. Leonard would sit in the back of the theater and watch as I rehearsed.

One evening, Joe brought my sister, Renee, and her husband to the theater. He told her that I'd be joining them shortly after the curtain went up—she had no idea I was studying to be an actress. The curtain rose in the darkened auditorium. When I walked onto the stage, I heard my sister's voice cry out in shock, "Joe, what is Estée *doing* up there??"

My acting career was short-lived, I'm afraid. I was not destined to be a Sarah Bernhardt, even though I did have a retentive memory.

Was I vain? There wasn't a minute of any day when I didn't look as pretty as I knew how to make myself. It was a matter of pride to me;

it was a matter of self-respect. There is no reason ever to look sloppy because it takes so little time to look wonderful.

Hair did take a little more time, I must admit. In my mother's day, beauty salons were not exactly dotting the main street. A young girl would come to our house to wash and brush Mother's hair (even though chances were I'd already brushed it twice that day already). Sometimes she'd even put in a few rag curlers, but not too many, since my mother's naturally curly hair was her pride and joy. Beauty, like medicine, was strictly a house-call profession in those days. Just think—hair dryers did not even exist.

Every time I think of hair dryers, I think of Elizabeth Arden—not a nice woman, not a generous woman. At her peak, she used to shampoo her own salon's carpeting and she brought her lunch to work every day in a brown paper bag. Not my style. She was subject to rages and fits of jealousy that were sometimes uncontrollable. If you were a professional threat, you were her enemy forever. Miss Arden called Charles Revson "that man" because she couldn't bear to address him by name. To annoy her, Revson brought out a men's perfume called That Man. Once, I was in Paris and in dreadful need of a hairdresser. Only the Elizabeth Arden Salon was open in Paris on Mondays. Swallowing my competitive spirit, I found myself under a dryer at her salon when the great woman herself walked in, spotted me, and marched over. I'd met her only briefly once before.

"Well, hello," I said. "So nice to see you again."

"Never mind," she said. "Why did you steal away my public relations lady?"

"I know nothing about it," I said. I didn't. Really.

"Well, now you do know about it and I don't want you here, either."

I got up, took the rollers out of my hair, picked up a nearby comb, ran it through my damp curls, paid my bill, and left. I never saw her again.

All this happened soon after Miss Arden had hired away virtually the whole of Helena Rubinstein's executive staff. Helena Rubinstein retaliated by hiring Miss Arden's ex-husband, Thomas Lewis.

THE HOUSE OF ASH BLONDES

When I was a young mother, there were hair dryers and I was grateful for them. One of my most pleasant pastimes was going once a month to the House of Ash Blondes, a beauty salon on West Seventy-second Street owned by Mrs. Florence Morris. There, I'd get my blondness renewed, my hair washed and marcelled, and I'd have an opportunity to chat with other young women in search of beauty.

Many of the young women who came to Florence Morris to get their hair done would come to my home for a quick beauty lesson. I loved sharing what I knew and creating excitement about skin! The only break in my busy day would be at lunchtime, when Leonard came home. There was always a hot lunch waiting to perk him up for his afternoon school activities. The women would wait. They understood.

One day Mrs. Morris said to me, "What do you do to keep your skin looking so fresh and lovely?"

It would turn out to be a question of great moment for me.

I didn't have to be asked twice. "The next time I come," I said, "I'll bring some of my products."

My heart was pounding. Although Mrs. Morris had asked a very innocent question, my mind began to race with a Great Idea. There are great ideas and Great Ideas.

In less than a month, earlier than my regular appointment time, I was back at the House of Ash Blondes with four jars, on which only *everything* rested.

"Would you mind leaving them with me?" she asked as I offered her my four products. "I'm so busy now. I'll try them when I have time, Mrs. Lauder."

I knew better. "Just let me show you how they work, Mrs. Morris,"

I said. "Give me just five minutes and you'll see the right way to use them."

Nothing could have induced me to leave my bounty without a demonstration. First I applied some extra fine Cleansing Oil to Mrs. Morris' face, then gently removed it. Then, before she could change her mind, I patted on my Creme Pack. Her face began to glow almost instantly. The Creme Pack, by the way, is still one of my biggest sellers. It doesn't harden like masques, which usually have to be scraped off. Instead, it can be removed easily with tissues. The original magic potion, my uncle's Super-Rich All Purpose Creme, followed. After tissuing that off, I applied a light skin lotion. Those were the staples of my repertoire. I brushed her face with the lightest and softest of face powders, which Uncle John and I had just developed, then on her cheeks and lips I used a bit of the new glow I had been testing.

Fini. I showed Mrs. Morris a mirror. She was a raving beauty.

Silence. She was thinking. "Do you think you would be interested in running the beauty concession at my new salon at 39 East Sixtieth Street?" she asked.

I did not hesitate a second. Up until that point, I had been giving away my products. This was my first chance at a real business. I would have a small counter in her store. I would pay her rent; whatever I sold would be mine to keep. No partners (I never did have partners). I would risk the rent, but if it worked, I would start the business I always dreamed about. Risk taking is the cornerstone of empires. No one ever became a success without taking chances. Yes, yes, yes, Mrs. Morris! I was interested.

First things first. If I was going to be in business, I needed proper jars. I rushed out to buy dozens of simple white opal-glass jars with black covers, which looked quite professional to me. My uncle had marketed creams under his wife's name, Floranna, but now it was my turn, and my business. I wanted to see my name in lights, but I was willing to settle for my name on a jar. It was a big decision. Josephine was my first name, but aside from the fact that no one called me by that name, it was too long for a jar label. Estée Lauder made her first public appearance on a little black-and-white container.

What follows is one of my typical beauty sessions at the salon.

A woman sitting under the dryer would be rather bored with the time it took to dry her hair. Her restlessness would work for me. I'd ask her to let me try a special cream on her face—free of charge. I promised it would make her skin feel pampered and soft, would make her skin feel silky. Of course, she would agree. She had nothing else to do under that dryer. When her hair had dried, but before it was combed out, I would remove the cream and quickly make up her face before she had a chance to think about it. First the glow (not hard rouge—my product *glowed*), then the Honey Glow powder with its own foundation base. Then a bit of turquoise eye shadow (I had read in a book that turquoise made the whites of the eyes look whiter and clearer). Finally, my Duchess Crimson lipstick, which made one's teeth seem like pearls. It was the most beautiful lipstick created. To be perfectly candid, it was the *only* shade I had. Did I know the Duchess of Windsor? I was asked. Was that lipstick named for her?

My response was always vague.

I would send the woman off to get combed out. When she was finished, the total look delighted her. "What did you do?" "What did you use?" "How did you do it?" was the inevitable barrage of questions.

Like Mrs. Morris, she had only to ask. I would supply her with a list of the products I used. In most cases, she would leave the salon with at least some of my creams and makeup.

SALES TECHNIQUE OF THE CENTURY

Now, the big secret: I would give the woman a sample of whatever she did not buy as a gift. It might be a few teaspoonfuls of powder in a wax envelope. Perhaps I'd shave a bit off the tip of a lipstick and tell her to apply it with her fingers. Perhaps, in still another envelope, I would give her a bit of glow. The point was this: a woman would never leave empty-handed. I did not have an advertising department. I did not have a copywriter, but I had a woman's intuition. I just knew, even though I had not yet named the technique, that a gift with a purchase was very appealing. In those days, I would even give a gift without a purchase. The idea was to convince a woman to try a product. Having tried it at her leisure in her own home and seeing how fresh and lovely it made her look, she would be faithful forever. Of that I had not one single doubt.

My clientele grew. One day a representative of the Albert and Carter Beauty Salon asked me to demonstrate my products there as well. I did some quick calculations in my head. If I could make $10 a day selling $2 worth of products to five women at one beauty shop, I could make $50 a day if I had five shops—an astronomical sum in those days. There was one problem. I could not be everywhere at once, and sales depended on my special approach. I had to expand, to delegate authority, but unless it was done my way, it would not work. I clearly had to train saleswomen.

About twenty young women responded to my advertisement in the newspaper. All of them watched as I began to make up one of them.

"You can use this wonderful all-purpose cream in the morning or in the evening. No going crazy with four separate creams! . . . This is one glow that will make you look so radiant you will not believe it . . . Note how I am shaking this powder before I apply it. Always shake powder to make it look light and airy, not matted and heavy, on your face. I always apply powder with a puff of sterile cotton, the most efficient way to do it . . ."

I completed the makeup, then asked each young woman to convince a "customer," who had just entered a salon, to be made up. I watched. Some were self-conscious, others too aggressive. Only a Miss Sari Roberts was wonderful. She had verve, she had conviction. She did not say, "May I help you?" knowing full well that the customer would not be in the store if she did not require assistance. Instead she said, "I have something that would look perfect on you, madam. May I show you how to apply it?"

Miss Roberts it was. She was with me for years.

I hired other saleswomen in the same way. I made it my business to check with each of them, each day, to make certain she was selling as I would. A devoted clientele was developing, not to my surprise, of course. My products were the finest. The beauty salon atmosphere was perfect—women were already in the self-improvement mood. Why should they go home with beautifully coiffed hair and a tired, lifeless face? It made sense to sell a total beauty package.

Word spread. Business moved gradually, but steadily. I worked every day from nine, when I arrived to polish my jars, to six in the evening. I never lunched. I felt I had to be there for every woman or I would surely lose her. On occasion a client would mention her daughter's skin problem and I would offer to help. A Creme Pack, a gentle glow, and her daughter's face acquired clarity after a few sessions. Believe it or not, transformations happened at Florence Morris.

One day a woman from Long Island came to the salon. Sophie Auerbach had the most dreadful skin imaginable. After three weeks of Creme Packs, her skin was almost clear and her spirits soaring. Before long, word spread to Philadelphia, where her brother owned a pharmacy. Florence Morris gained a loyal Pennsylvania following, not to mention the matrons of Long Island who, lured by Sophie's testimonials, made the trek to New York. I cleansed, creamed, colored, talked, talked, talked, and talked. The big seller was the Creme Pack, even though it smelled awful in those days (and that smell is not vastly improved even today, I must admit). It worked like a charm, and the interest in my line grew. Customers were beginning to call department stores looking for my products, and I could not have been more pleased by that development.

Once a woman from St. Louis told me her son had problem adolescent skin and was suffering great embarrassment. He would not use her Creme Pack, no matter how she implored, because it was "woman's stuff." I ran around the corner, bought a perfectly plain jar, poured in my Creme Pack, and instructed the woman to tell her son it had come from a skin specialist. I was not surprised to hear that the boy's skin improved considerably. My uncle's formula was definitely unisex.

MOVING ON

Quite by accident I discovered an eager audience waiting for me in the fine hotels of Long Island. During a short vacation I'd made up a few women at poolside. The response was electric. In the next few years I'd spend some weeks alone at the Lido or Grand Hotel on what might be dubbed working vacations. Many women would gather and ask me to teach them about skin care and cosmetics. It was fun for them and profitable for me. I dressed as they did, as elegantly as I knew how. In my day there were no courses on dressing for success, but *I knew I had to look my best to sell my best*. The hotel owners welcomed the diversion I provided. It cost them nothing, and my services were more enthusiastically received than an entertainer's. Women wanted to learn, not laugh at silly jokes. One summer after another, I pushed myself, lauding creams, making up women, selling beauty. In the winters, I'd visit these eager ladies at their homes, where, with a bridge game as a backdrop, I'd make up their friends and sell more creams. The mood at these sessions was as exhilarating for me as for them.

I didn't need bread to eat, but I worked as though I did . . . from pure love of the venture. For me, teaching about beauty was and is an emotional experience. I brought them charisma and knowledge about their possibilities. They gave me a sense of success. I felt flushed with excitement after each session. Pure theater—in the end that's what it was, this rendering of beauty. Pure theater for me!

Traveling, moving from group to group, hotel to hotel, trying to build what I was coming to see as an extraordinary future, I spent less and less time at home. Indeed, I was away so much that I lost touch with what was most important to me.

MOVING APART

Now I shall speak of a time of great pain, great confusion. It's difficult for me to speak of it. I'm always reluctant to divulge intimate family matters, but I've determined to be candid in this book, and so I shall. I suppose what I will now say will shock even many of my close friends, because it involves a secret shared with almost no one—until this moment.

Success and exhilaration don't always bring wisdom. I am a visceral person by nature. I act on instinct, quickly, without pondering possible disaster and without indulging in deep introspection. This quality can work well in the business world, where instinct counts and where one must be able to risk and take immediate action, but the same quality can be an irritant in personal relationships. I was moving steadily forward, and all the progress brought with it a great deal of activity that neither interested nor, in many ways, included Joe, in part because of his quieter nature. Many of my contacts were social. At the drop of a hat, I'd invite a prospective buyer to our home for dinner, or, without a moment's thought, I'd make an appointment to dine out. My husband preferred a less frenetic life. I loved a party; he would far prefer dining at home, listening to the radio, reading. I wanted to talk with others; he, in the early days, was happier talking only with me. We both yearned for success but had very different ways of seeking it. Being young, we were not accomplished in compromise. Deep, deep in my heart I loved him so much, but I was impatient and moving ahead faster than he. Joe was solid and serene. I was quicksilver and driven.

It's not that we had a stressful marriage in those early days. He was always my confidant, always my trusted ally. His wry sense of humor put the intensity of my concerns in perspective. His quips were memorable. "We compromise," he once said to friends who asked about our social life. "I go where she goes. We always compromise like that." Or, "No, of course we don't go out that much. Just six nights a week."

He observed a lovely formality in our relationship that lasted all our lives. When I entered a room, he'd always put his newspaper aside, sometimes even stand up, and always, always he'd stop what he was doing to listen to me.

But I just couldn't do the same for him at that point in our lives. When he wanted to talk, I'd usually be off in another world, thinking, projecting, planning, my thoughts on a dozen projects, my mind awhirl. Although I felt I'd always known Joe, I didn't have the concentration to *build* on that closeness. I was busy building a business.

He was very wonderful and very patient.

I was not so wonderful and very patient. And too young and inexperienced to recognize what I had. A jewel. Priceless. My perfect balance.

For longer and longer periods of time, I was traveling to hotels, leaving Joe at home with Leonard and a maid. I was single-minded in the pursuit of my dream. He was having business difficulties.

"What's this all about," he'd say to me. "Why do we really need this?"

And I'd answer, "Don't worry, one day it will all be fine."

"But when is 'one day' going to come?" he'd ask.

"I don't know," had to be the response. "Soon."

It couldn't be soon enough for him. People were referring to Joe as Mr. Estée Lauder. He didn't like it at all.

Here is a lesson I have learned: whether you are a businesswoman or housewife, attention must be paid to your mate. If a marriage is to succeed, whether or not a man is successful in his chosen field, whether or not a woman is, she must take exquisite care to make her man feel strong and important—and then he will *be* strong and important. Let's hope he does the same for her. Success, happiness, contentment, are self-fulfilling prophecies. This is a lesson I learned, and there was grief in the learning.

Joe was ambitious, as I was, but his ambitions weren't fulfilled immediately. After graduating from the High School of Commerce, where he had studied accounting, he became a salesman for a silk company. Soon after he started his own business—the Apex Silk Company—which imported the finest fabrics. The timing was wrong, however. The country was on the brink of a depression, and because the price of silk rose sharply, business profits sank sadly. Joe felt frustration. He tried a number of other ventures, but despite his brilliant mind, his absolute knack for numbers and organization, he couldn't fight the country's belt tightening. He was intimidated also by a young wife with an appetite for excitement. I wanted too much, too soon. There was no doubt about it. Tensions at home began to grow.

Do remember, I was married very young. I had seen so little of the world. When I started meeting attractive people in my business, and when I'd dress up and feel pretty, daring, and desirable—well, it was as invigorating as a roller-coaster ride. Joe just could not understand that roller coaster. Extremes of living and emotion had little to do with his more reserved nature but were natural for me.

So many small things were sources of strain. The details that mattered to me were often unimportant to Joe. I was not only moving farther ahead than he, but I was doing so in a world he did not share. I did not know how to be Mrs. Joseph Lauder and Estée Lauder at the same time.

We bickered. We made up. One day, at a party, I forgot to introduce Joe to the other guests. Everyone knew me; no one knew him. He was hurt and offended by my lapse. I was exasperated. Why didn't he introduce himself? We were, in short, having problems that both of us were too immature to deal with. Feminism was almost unheard of then. There were no guidelines to help a strong woman live happily with a much loved but gentler man.

My mother went to Florida for a short stay, and soon after, I followed her. In Florida, life was very lighthearted. I made friends with people who were experimenting with their own lives. In retrospect, I know that most of them were not friends at all. Some were jealous of my success, my clothes, my family; some were just troublemakers. I was very vulnerable.

One woman, a very mischievous new divorcée, said to me over and over again, ''Estée, you're foolish. You're young and beautiful and stuck with a husband who doesn't understand you. If you were smart, you'd divorce him. It's so easy to do it here! Start a whole new life . . .''

Perhaps in many couples' lives there comes a time when some apartness, some separation, is necessary to make both stronger. It seemed as if this was true in my marriage. I filed for divorce in Florida. Joe was heartsick, but after many, many impassioned conversations, he complied. It was 1939 when we officially parted.

But we were never really apart. I was ostensibly a free woman, but I saw my ex-husband often. He was, after all, my best friend. We had our adored son. We had our inescapable deep love. For a while I had gay and giddy fun—dressing up, going out on dates, flirting outrageously. There were some romantic interludes, in the true sense of the word—romantic. Impassioned affairs were out of the question in my world in the forties. Sexual freedom was decades away.

There was one man who captured my imagination in the years that Joe and I were apart. He was Charles Moskowitz, an executive of Metro-Goldwyn-Mayer. He courted me in a lovely, old-fashioned way. He showed me a world I'd never even imagined . . . Hollywood, stardom, glitter! We went to theater openings and movie premieres. I even saw a very young Frank Sinatra audition for Charles. I felt the wave of electricity that shot through everyone who listened to the slender, earnest young man with the most romantic voice I'd ever heard. Though the life was glamorous, I caught myself thinking of Joe and wishing I could share some of the new, fascinating things I was seeing with him. Too often, I caught myself thinking of Joe.

I would be seen on the arms of various business associates, who were perfect escorts. Those friendships were purely business on my part, but

I'm sure it must have looked otherwise to those who might have observed from afar. They didn't know me very well. Business itself was the purest romance for me.

For a few years I found myself free, doing all the things young girls do now before they marry. I had come directly from my parents' house to a life that included a husband and, very quickly, a child. My parents had insisted upon the European form of marriage making. Dating, experimenting, and just having fun were never options for me. My parents were old-world, and no daughter of theirs would consider attachments to men before marriage.

Undeniably, the new freedom after my divorce was diverting. It was not satisfying. I kept needing to tell Joe something funny that had happened. I had him on my mind too much. In a sea of new experiences and people, I was lonely. I missed the gentle solidness of the darling man I'd married in the first place.

Leonard says he remembers Joe's visits to Florida and his presence in New York. He remembers crying bitterly whenever his father had to leave because he so loved Joe. I remember the tears as well. They broke my heart.

We'd carefully told our young son not that we were divorcing or even separating but that "Daddy is going to sleep closer to the business," and not with Mommy anymore. That was something Leonard could understand. At the time, being closer to the business took precedence over everything.

The loneliness grew worse and worse. It was becoming unbearable. Joe, Leonard, and I craved family. We were, above all, family people.

MOVING AS ONE

Four years passed. One day Leonard began to run a high fever, then showed signs of having the mumps. Joe came immediately and stayed all afternoon to worry with me and to read to Leonard. Toward evening,

Leonard improved wonderfully. I remember that his face shone with the joy of having both his parents in the same house.

For the first time in years, Joe stayed the night. We shared the same room. The following night he was still there, and the following.

On the fourth night Joe sat me down in the living room. "Estée, what are we doing to ourselves?" he asked. "We should be together."

I thought long and hard. What *am* I doing to myself? I have a man who loves me and whom I love in every important way. We have a child. We trust each other. I can't go on without this man by my side.

"I know I made a great mistake," I told him. "Forgive me."

We kissed.

There were no canes this time, no calla lilies, no picture in the rotogravure. Instead, we went to City Hall in 1943. Our marriage was to become, for me at any rate, one of the greatest love stories of all time.

Many years later, President Nixon sounded me out to see if I'd be interested in being ambassador to Luxembourg. I was so excited! Just imagine, little Estée from Queens—an ambassador!

I was overwhelmed.

"If you go, you go alone," said Joe that night. "I won't go along to carry your bags."

That was it for being ambassador. No one ever accused me of not learning important lessons.

Our second wedding ceremony was profoundly important and moving. Our recemented bonds were unbreakable. We were never to be separated for longer than a few days ever again. We always, till the day he died, the blackest, saddest day of my life, had each other to hold. To talk to.

A member of the British royal family once said to me, "I am so happy since my marriage. Everyone needs someone to talk to in the still, dark hours."

I've never forgotten those words because they are so very true. During the years I was apart from Joe, in one way I had a heady, exciting time, but I'll always remember coming home at night and not having that one, sweet, trusted someone with whom to share my deep thoughts, my secrets. You cannot fly on one wing.

I feel compelled to tell you what I've learned about divorce.

It's far too easy to say goodbye in America. In so many cases, when women marry again, they only change the face, not the problems. Too many divorced friends find that their second husband, or even their third husband, has more faults than their first husband, who looks better and better on someone else's arm. I always try to talk people out of divorcing. People divorce these days as fast as they change hair color.

So Joe and I were remarried, this time forever—but with a few changes. First of all, my primary identity would be Mrs. Joseph Lauder, not Estée Lauder. Second of all, we decided that Joseph would give up his business and come into mine, where we would be equal partners in every sense of the word. We would work together: he would deal with the economics and practical aspects of the business, I would do the selling. It couldn't have happened at all without Joe . . . and his head for figures. Every time I wanted to spend money, he'd hold me back. I spent it anyway, but if I didn't have him there saying, "No, no, don't do it," I'd have spent a fatal amount. I counted money differently. What I saw as Gifts With Purchase or Beautiful Packaging, he saw as Expenses. I had no head for expenses—only for profits. When I was on the road, I spoke to Joe every night. I knew I needed him not only for emotional support but also to keep me in line financially.

After a year, we cemented our new bonds with a new child, our brilliant and sensitive son Ronald, who was born in February 1944. Our family was complete, our lives were sweeter, and our future was clear.

A SECRET WEAPON

But nothing happened fast. Many stories have surrounded the growth of big business, certainly my big business, and most of them are myths.

The most insidious myth of all is the one that promises magic formulas and instant success. It does not happen that way. I cried more than I ate. There was constant work, constant attention to detail, lost hours of sleep, worries, heartaches. Friends and family didn't let a day go by without discouraging us.

"Estée, what do you need this for? Stay home with your darling family . . ." They meant well. Despite all the nay sayers, there was never a single moment when I considered giving up. That was simply not a viable alternative. I had a secret weapon. There were, in those days before television and high-gloss advertising, only two key ways to communicate a message quickly. They were: telephone and telegraph.

I had a third. It was potent: Tell-a-Woman.

Women were telling women. They were selling my cream before they even got to my salon. Tell-a-Woman was the word-of-mouth campaign that launched Estée Lauder Cosmetics.

Joe and I allowed ourselves to become excited. It was time to consider our next step. Ironically, as we began to feel soaringly optimistic, the economy was foundering. Men were desperately searching for work. Their wives, no longer shopping in the department stores, would still manage to stop into Florence Morris for a shot of confidence-building beauty.

"There's no business, no business at all," moaned the newspapers.

But I knew there was business in beauty as long as there was a woman alive. We have to eat 365 days a year. We get dressed every day. Women take care of their faces with the same consistency. Business is always there if one looks for it. A woman in those hard times would first feed her children, then her husband, but she would skip her own lunch to buy a fine face cream.

I decided to try another saleswoman in a Brooklyn beauty salon, but I soon discovered that Brooklyn was just too far away for me to control the situation. I had to supervise, had to be involved. Every day I touched fifty faces.

My father was so unhappy. "Estée, all that touching . . ." he would mutter in distress.

The time was fast approaching when I would enlist his help. Horatio Alger notwithstanding, almost no one starts from scratch. Though I have read repeatedly that "Estée Lauder built a fortune from nothing," the assertion is wrong, wrong, wrong. Do not let the Pollyannas mislead you. One simply cannot start from zero. If you want to start your own business, save some money or know someone who can lend you some. You may not need a huge amount, but those first bills must be covered— and then some. When I began, business practice was based on CBD— cash before delivery—not COD. The same holds true in many cases today.

The American dream is powerfully enticing, but it is a dream. One does not move from rags—poof—to riches by dreaming or by starting from zero. Henry Ford did begin building cars in a wooden shed with a door too small to allow the car through, but I guarantee he had *some* money to buy the shed or even the parts for the car. One could say that Estée Lauder Cosmetics started in a stable, but there was a lovely house in front of that tiny stable and a father with some means who had confidence in his daughter. Hard work, ingenuity, and inspiration are unquestionably important, but so is a little help, or a little savings— Joe's savings, I might add.

"Papa, I know how to do it," I would assure my worried father. "They're coming from all over to buy my creams. I have ideas that no one else ever had."

He knew it was so, even though his refrain was, "When is this going to end?"

LABEL TROUBLE

We needed cash on the line to pay for paper shipping boxes that we had bought—I remember as if it were yesterday—from A. Dorfman and

Company. We needed cash on the line for the production ingredients. We needed cash on the line for the new jars. All CBD.

Why new jars? Well, to be honest, the white opal-glass jars with the black caps looked a bit medicinal. I was selling pure glamour, and it had to be dressed for the part.

And then there was that dreadful business with the pasted labels.

My friend Mrs. Nevins was the wife of the owner of a huge department store on Fourteenth Street in New York. She loved my Super-Rich All Purpose Creme. One day she told me that she was planning a trip of several months' duration. "Could I take along some of those handy four-ounce jars?" she asked.

The answer was certainly, but since preservatives were not perfected in those days and all my ingredients were pure and natural, I told her to keep the jars in her refrigerator until departure to keep the cream as fresh as possible.

Mrs. Nevins gave a farewell dinner before she left. Her maid set about preparing the salad and dressing. Dampness from the refrigerator had caused the labels of my Super-Rich All Purpose Creme to peel off the jars, and the chill from the refrigerator made the oil rise to the top of each jar.

Mrs. Nevins' maid wondered why the mayonnaise tasted so odd—not *bad*, mind you—just odd. A little more vinegar, a little more salt and pepper, and the salad dressing seemed just fine.

After the party Mrs. Nevins wandered into the kitchen and saw the Super-Rich All Purpose Creme jars standing, label-less and empty, on her kitchen counter.

"Not mayonnaise?" the maid repeated in disbelief. "Then what did I put in the salad dressing?"

"Will my people die?" a frantic Mrs. Nevins asked me on the phone at two in the morning.

"Nonsense, my dear, of course they won't," I reassured her. "Pull yourself together. There are only pure products in that cream—it's probably healthier than mayonnaise. Go to sleep. You'll see, tomorrow everyone will call to say how delicious your dinner was!"

They did, of course. Mrs. Nevins told me she could never again use my cream on her face—it reminded her of mayonnaise. Nor could she ever again eat mayonnaise. It tasted suspiciously like Super-Rich All Purpose Creme.

So the jars and the untrustworthy labels had to go. The new jars would be a decision of detail that could affect the entire business. I knew I had to make the right decision.

ESTÉE LAUDER BLUE

First of all, I reasoned, where would my jars sit? In every woman's bathroom, naturally. Second, I knew that I wanted every woman to remember whose cream it was that was making her look so fresh and lovely; that excluded labels that came off in shower-generated steam. The name would have to be embedded right on the jar. Needless to say, the jar had to be beautiful. And this was the hard part—it couldn't clash with my customers' bathroom decors.

At the time, T. C. Wheaton was the company that specialized in the finest glass containers. Having obtained sample jars, my research consisted of matching the few colors to which I had narrowed my choices to wallpapers in every guest bathroom I could manage to visit. I would fill my evening purse with a few small sample jars. Every time I went to a friend's home or even an elegant restaurant, I'd excuse myself from the company, visit the bathroom, and match my jar colors against a vast array of wallpapers. There were silver bathrooms, purple bathrooms, black and white bathrooms, brown bathrooms, gold bathrooms, pink bathrooms—even red bathrooms. Which color would look wonderful in any bathroom? I deliberated for weeks. I spent an inordinate amount of time "freshening up." People must have worried about my long absences from the company. Finally, I had it. There was a single, delicate, different, cool color I had loved from the first. It wasn't blue, it wasn't green. It was somewhere in between—a fragile, pale turquoise that was memorable. It was also perfect with every wallpaper, in the grandest of homes as well as in the most modest. I knew that women would not buy cosmetics in garish containers that offended their bathroom decor: I wanted them to be proud to display my products. The jars had to send a message of luxury and harmony. They had to be unique. A great package does not copy or study. It invents.

(Twenty years later, Estée Lauder blue was the color of thousands and thousands of extravagant flowers that filled the La Scala Opera House in Milan, Italy, when I was the guest of honor at the opening festivities. It was a *very* nice color.)

In the meantime, Florence Morris and the other salons were filled with my Tell-a-Woman customers.

"Madam, won't you please let me show you how this finest of creams, made from only pure ingredients, can make your complexion glow with youth and radiance? It will only take two minutes . . ." Who could resist? As it turned out, no one. Each woman received small gifts and precise directions on how to use the cosmetics. Today, I walk into large department stores and see every cosmetic company in the world giving free demonstrations because they have learned from me that showing counts more than telling. If I could just apply my products to a woman's face, she would see the difference and she would *have* to have them. I began to realize I had a priceless gift—the ability to make friends and convince others of my sincerity. I know I could not sell a product that was not effective. On the other hand, I could sell coals to Newcastle if I was persuaded that my coals were stellar.

I was beginning to feel restless with the success I was enjoying at the salons. It soon became apparent that I needed to have a larger marketplace—the great department stores to be exact—partly because of the new phenomenon of charge accounts. At the beauty salon, a woman would have to pay for merchandise with cash; this precluded impulse buying, that is, making a spontaneous purchase when she had no intention of spending money and had not brought extra money with her. My customers asked me repeatedly, "Do you have a counter at Saks Fifth Avenue where I could charge?" Though the answer was no, I knew I would soon have to transform that into a solid *yes*. Saks, then and now, represents one of the most elegant, the finest of shopping places. I resolved to break the rules that sheltered this traditional and exclusive store from experimental merchandisers who would sell their souls to sell from Saks.

BREAKTHROUGH

My name was not exactly unknown there. The Tell-a-Woman campaign had already resulted in hundreds of phone calls from women asking for my products. The store was beginning to wonder about me. Then good fortune arrived in the guise of two different women. Miss Marion Coombs, an assistant buyer at Saks, had been injured in an automobile accident, which left her skin unpleasantly scarred. I gave her some treatments with my Creme Pack, and after several weeks we were both delighted to see a fine improvement. Soon afterward another young woman, who happened to be the daughter of a Saks Fifth Avenue executive, came in to see me. She was wearing a little veil over troubled and reddened skin. Again, with a few treatments, her skin began to clear up beautifully. Word spread among the powers who make big decisions at Saks Fifth Avenue. At the same time, the enthusiastic phone calls from my own clients were having an effect.

It came to pass one day that Mr. Robert Fisk, the cosmetics buyer at Saks and one of the nicest men, acceded to my millionth request. He gave me a small order for approximately $800 worth of merchandise. Hallelujah! We were in business in a big way. We closed down our counters at Florence Morris and at Albert and Carter to concentrate on Saks. As the icing on the cake, the wonderful director of advertising believed wholeheartedly in my products. We decided to send to my own customers and all those people with charge accounts at Saks a small, elegant white printed card with gold lettering that read, "Saks Fifth Avenue is proud to present the Estée Lauder line of cosmetics: now available at our cosmetics department."

Did we have a hundred wonderful treatment products? No. We had four. They were Super-Rich All Purpose Creme, Cleansing Oil, Creme Pack, and Skin Lotion. Only four products, but they could have been made of pure gold! We also had a select few cosmetic products. Our Gift With Purchase was a small sample of cream-based face powder.

Joe and I knew we had to start running a very different, much more serious operation; space became the operative word. We set about finding our first "factory" to fill our new, terribly momentous Saks Fifth Avenue order. They were the first, the very first, to take us on and I would never forget it. Ever since, I've had a special place in my heart for this store: breaking that first, mammoth barrier was perhaps the single most exciting moment I have ever known.

Fortunately, our confidence equaled our excitement, because we had to have enough faith in our work to invest all our savings.

Our first home base was a former restaurant on Central Park West— 1 West Sixty-fourth Street. We had to pay six months' rent in advance. Those were potent words—"in advance"—but we swallowed hard and signed. On the restaurant's gas burners we cooked our creams, mixed them, sterilized our pretty new jars with boiling water, poured and filled and planned and packaged. We did everything ourselves. I still have one of those gas burners, which I treasure as a memento of our beginnings. Every bit of work was done by hand—four hands, Joe's and mine. We had my uncle's original cream and others I'd created by then. We stayed up all night for nights on end, snatching sleep in fits and starts. The order for Saks had to be produced on time. As D-day (delivery day) loomed, we hired a man to help us, and deliver we did—on time. At last, we were in the big leagues of business. For years I had been giving away my merchandise. When someone once asked Joseph what business we were in during the beauty-salon era, he replied, "The giveaway business. It does very well."

"Don't you worry," I recall telling him, "whatever we give away, God will give back to us."

And that is the way it happened. All the people to whom I had given samples, all the people who had been telling other people, all those people appeared on opening day at Saks Fifth Avenue.

In two days, we were sold out. The fun was about to start. And with that came the endless work, the endless traveling, the endless streams, rivers, tides, torrents, oceans of words I would utter in praise of the products I knew were the creams of the crop. I was a woman with a mission. I had to show as many women as I could reach not only how to be beautiful, but how to stay beautiful. On the way, I hoped in my secret heart to find fame and fortune.

It was 1946.

CHAPTER 3

ON THE ROAD

It was 101° in the shade in downtown San Antonio, Texas, and I was making my first personal appearance at the Estée Lauder counter in the elegant Frost Brothers Department Store.

Slowly a woman made her way toward us. She was short, swarthy, and definitely out of her element—that much was clear. For a moment all eyes were riveted upon her. I just knew it had taken great personal courage for the Mexican woman to get this far. For one thing, she wore no shoes. For another, she had two gold teeth where the snowy smiles of the other shoppers shone. What could Frost Brothers hold for her? What made her chance this unfamiliar terrain?

In a moment it was clear. She stopped directly in front of the counter and gazed wistfully at the gleaming jars.

Large pores, I thought to myself.

Then she pointed to one jar and looked up expectantly. I was about to assist her when the salesperson tapped me on the shoulder. "Not her, Mrs. Lauder," she whispered. "Don't waste your time. She's not going to buy anything. I know her type. I live around here."

I remember whirling around to tap the salesperson on her own shoulder. "Since when do you know how much money she has in her pocketbook?" I asked quietly.

The Mexican woman brightened as she saw me approach. She pointed again to the Super-Rich Moisturizing Creme. Good taste. I liked that woman.

I went to work. First the Cleansing Oil, which I patted on and immediately tissued off. Then the Creme Pack, which I left on for a minute, then removed. I applied just a bit of my Super-Rich All Purpose Creme, worked it in, and removed the excess. Then I brushed a bit of blusher on her cheeks to give definition to her round face, patted on some powder, added just a touch of Duchess Crimson lipstick—and handed her a mirror.

She stared and stared, then smiled. Her strong and gracious face, set off by a gloriously hued serape, was positively radiant. She couldn't speak English. I couldn't speak Spanish. Still, at that moment I felt such a bond with that woman as she and I both marveled at the miracles of twentieth-century makeup.

You know the ending to this story before I write it. She opened her sagging black purse. It was literally overflowing with dollars—not a sign of a peso anywhere. She bought two of everything I'd used on her face, and the next day her relatives did the same.

I never forgot her. She symbolized so much for me. Never be patronizing, never underestimate *any* woman's desire for beauty. That proud woman embodies my whole philosophy. I would be on the road for the rest of my life, in a way, always touching faces, always making the sale that others said was impossible.

LIFE LESSON

I'd felt so exhilarated from the Saks success, almost as if I was riding my childhood horse, Bessie, at a fast gallop. A slow trot was more like it, and it took every effort to keep even that modest pace going. It would be so easy to lose ground if I let up for just a moment.

We had little experience and no guidelines about whom to trust and whom not to trust in our business relationships. And sometimes we made the wrong choice. As in the box-maker incident.

We decided to try a new box-manufacturing concern. Operating on the CBD principle, we paid for our merchandise in advance. The company did not deliver. We called and pleaded and threatened, but the concern kept the down payment and the boxes as well.

I remember going as a family to Long Island City to plead in person with the manager to ship the boxes or to return our money. Without resolution, we'd be out of business before we really started. Somehow we convinced the manager to deliver those essential boxes. The expedition remains so vivid in Leonard's memory for its frustration that more than thirty years later he still speaks of the lesson he learned that day.

"When a person with experience meets a person with money," says Leonard whenever you remind him of the day, "pretty soon, the person with the experience will have the money and the person with the money will have the experience."

It was, in retrospect, a good lesson to learn—even though we learned it painfully.

A NEW YEAR, A NEW FACE

The next prestige store I decided to take by storm was Neiman-Marcus in Dallas. Mr. Ben Eisner, the store's merchandise manager, was less than optimistic. "There's no room for a new counter," he intoned. "It's a bad time of the year. Give me a call when you can. We'll talk again."

I called and I called. I went to see him. It was always a bad time. There never was enough room.

One day, I suppose in deference to my profound eagerness, my refusal to be put off, and my insistence that was getting dangerously close to nagging, Mr. Eisner said that he could probably give me some room to open up on the day after New Year's. Not that he was encouraging. "No one will come out," he said. "It's just too hot. Besides, every woman will have spent all her money on Christmas. Don't get your hopes up."

That's just where they were. Up.

"Is there a local radio program I could go on?" I asked. "Just get me a fifteen-minute spot on the radio the day before we open," I begged. Mr. Eisner reluctantly agreed to do what he could.

The sun rose early, yellow and hot, on New Year's Day. I was primed to go on a local woman's program at 8:15 A.M. The time was available because only a minuscule audience was expected to be listening to the radio at that ungodly hour.

"Good morning, ladies," I practically sang into the microphone, as the sleepy-eyed technicians watched lethargically. "I'm Estée Lauder just in from Europe with the newest ideas for beauty. In this weather you have to work hard to look your loveliest, and I have the secrets. I have an all-purpose cream that takes the place of the four creams you've been using, and I have a glow and a powder that will make you look fresh and clean no matter how hot it is. *And* I have a small gift for every woman who comes in. Do let me personally show you how to accomplish the newest beauty tricks from Paris and London. Start the New Year with a new face."

Start the New Year with a new face. The women responded with verve—my counter overflowed with customers, my heart overflowed with joy. Neiman-Marcus ran the ad every year for all the years that followed: START THE NEW YEAR WITH A NEW FACE . . . ESTÉE LAUDER COSMETICS.

GROUND RULES

At this opening, this magnificent success, I set my own ground rules for the openings of Estée Lauder counters to come—all over the world, in every major department store, in every climate, in every neighborhood. My basic premises were never to falter. I had never taken a course in merchandising, but it all seemed quite clear to me.

First, I would open each store myself. I might have to travel by bus, train, or donkey, but I'd be there for a week to train the salespeople, to set out the merchandise attractively, to create the aura. My creams, my makeup, had the purest, most extraordinary ingredients. I had to convince the customer to try the products, and then she'd come to love them. We were selling jars of hope. If my customer couldn't buy a new dress this year, she could always buy one next year. But a new face—that she couldn't buy. She had to pay attention to her face, *right now*. My convictions were solid, and my strongest one was that I had to be everywhere *in person* to convince.

Second, I needed a special kind of salesperson. She had to look wonderful herself. She had to use my products and sell their effectiveness by example. I was not out to fool the customer. No one could tell her, and make her believe, that a certain cream would make her sexy, brilliant, or rich. What a cream could do was to make her clean, pretty, and confident. That was the truth. Confidence breeds beauty. The spokespeople for my products would always have to be smiling, pretty, and confident; very elegant, very soft and very fine. They couldn't be T and T salesgirls either. T and T salesgirls were always on the telephone or the toilet. Bad business. I needed my counter attended by alert, interested, eager young women. If a customer looks around for two minutes for a salesperson, finds no one available, another product will instantly catch her eye and you've lost her, perhaps forever.

The saleswoman was my most important asset. I knew it then. I know it now. She has to be a walking advertisement. She can't oversell—no woman ever appreciates being sold more than she needs. Actually, the saleswoman's job was not to sell, but to let women buy. She had to respect the customer. She had to know the product and believe in it. She had to know how to use it and what one could realistically expect from it. Most of all, she had to convince the customer to try it on, as she would a dress or hat. Then, and only then, would she make her sale.

Years later, the Duchess of Windsor would say to me, "Estée, your cream just puts a girdle around my face." I had convinced her to try it and that's how she knew. For now, en route to the Duchess, I had to convince the belles of Dallas.

Ambience counted deeply. Counters had to attract. Each Estée Lauder counter, I decided, would be a tiny, shining spa—complete. I'd make sure there was color to make them attractive. The color I chose was the same, wonderful, in-between-a-blue-and-a-green that whispered elegance, aristocracy, and also complemented bathroom wallpapers.

Finally the lure, the reason to appear at my counter, was the gift to the customer—the free something that would sell everything else. It sounds so simple, doesn't it? I'd have to agree. It *was* simple. Most good ideas sparkle in simplicity, so much so that everyone wonders why no one ever did that before.

Actually, the sample was the most honest way to do business. You give people a product to try. If they like its quality, they buy it. They haven't been lured by an advertisement but convinced by the product itself. Not that we never tried to go the advertising route in the beginning. Why wouldn't we? We tried everything.

We had asked a friend to recommend an advertising agency. BBD and O wasn't interested. They wouldn't take us on. No one would. We had far too little money to spend—nothing, in their minds.

We decided to go back to the samples. We took the money we had planned to use on advertising and invested it instead in enough material to give away large quantities of our products. It was so simple that our competitors sneered when they heard what we were doing. Today, even the banks are copying us.

GIFTS BY MAIL

The radio spot was the vehicle that announced the gift at Neiman-Marcus. I believe we were the very first cosmetics company to offer a free gift by mail. As business progressed in the other stores, we decided to send postcards directly to customers that read, "Madam, because you're one of our preferred customers, please stop by the Estée Lauder counter and present this card to get a free gift." It was a direct way to get people to try us. Today, mailing lists are *de rigueur,* but in those days no one thought of personally contacting the customer, who was faceless and addressless.

Direct mailing seems, in retrospect, to be a natural outgrowth of our Gift With Purchase technique, but it didn't happen quite so simply. We worked and worked to find a way to offer our cosmetics to customers in the most effective way, an approach more personal than offering a free gift via newspaper advertisement. It sounds like an accident, but inspirations don't fall from the sky. As Louis Pasteur once said, "Chance favors the prepared mind."

Incidentally, the merchandise we gave and give away is our prime merchandise, the best, the top of our line. Later, many other companies jumped on our bandwagon to offer gifts, but what they were giving away were their mistakes—the colors that didn't sell last season, the ineffective creams that died on the counter, last year's failures. They tried to unload their lemons on customers; many still do. Bad business, I say. How can you expect a customer to return for more if you've given your worst, even for free?

Before they copied me, they scoffed. Once, an executive of Charles of the Ritz walked into Lord & Taylor, put a giveaway travel-sized box of powder in his pocket, and quietly said to the buyer, "She'll never get ahead. She's giving away the whole business." Well, today Squibb owns Charles of the Ritz, and I'm still very much around, still "giving away" my business.

PERSISTENCE PAYS OFF

Business is not something to be lightly tried on, flippantly modeled. It's not a distraction, not an affair, not a momentary fling. Business marries you. You sleep with it, eat with it, think about it much of your time. It is, in a very real sense, an act of love. If it isn't an act of love, it's merely work, not business.

What makes a successful businesswoman? Is it talent? Well, perhaps, although I've known many enormously successful people who were not gifted in any outstanding way, not blessed with particular talent. Is it, then, intelligence? Certainly, intelligence helps, but it's not necessarily education or the kind of intellectual reasoning needed to graduate from the Wharton School of Business that are essential. How many of your grandfathers came here from one or another "old country" and made a mark in America without the language, money, or contacts? What, then, is the mystical ingredient?

It's persistence. It's that certain little spirit that compels you to stick it out just when you're at your most tired. It's that quality that forces you to persevere, find the route around the stone wall. It's the immovable stubbornness that will not allow you to cave in when everyone says give up.

On a rainy evening, just before we decided to commit ourselves to cosmetics full time, our accountant and our lawyer took us out to dinner. They had something grave to tell us. Joe and I thought it was important enough to include Leonard, quite young at the time, but responsible and eager to share in our decisions. We three and the two wise professionals sat down at the table.

"Don't do it," was the advice. "The mortality rate in the cosmetics industry is high, and you'll rue the day you invested your savings and your time into this impossible business. Estée and Joe, we beg of you, don't do it."

We did it. Today Leonard is fond of saying, and I agree, that "accountants and lawyers make great accountants and lawyers. We need them, but we make the business decisions." No one else. We make them. Mark Twain once said something like "Keep away from people who try to belittle your ambitions. Small people always do that. But the really great make you feel that you too can become great."

Our first year's sales amounted to about $50,000. Expenses ate up just about every dime. No matter. Forward.

There was a stone wall in my path after my successes at Saks and Neiman-Marcus, and I was determined to leap over it, or at the very least, tiptoe around it. Making individual contacts to gain entry into department stores was a solid way to do business, but it took too long. First, you had to establish a relationship with the cosmetics buyer—and that could take weeks, months, sometimes years—to convince him or her of your product's worth, then wait until room at the store was available. I started late. I didn't have the time for waiting, nor, I guess, the disposition. By the way, it is never too late to start a business, you know, just as it is never too late to make yourself beautiful. Women of a certain age are seasoned enough to bypass certain frivolities, certain temptations. They can focus on their interests more steadily than their youthful counterparts. It takes a certain tunnel vision, the ability to look directly ahead until the daylight is in sight. Older women are not quite as easily distracted. Whether they've decided to improve their faces or their fortunes, women are usually more successful when, believe it or not, they have an advantage of years.

My immediate problem was to find a way to make contact with many stores simultaneously. Miracle of miracles, I learned about buying offices. Have you ever noticed that when you're concentrating with passion on a project, you start hearing or reading about things germane to that project? Perhaps it's because your antennae are up, but I always considered it fascinating to note how the world around me responds to my particular current interests.

A buying office was what I needed, a central bureau that purchases for many stores throughout the country. Through its influence, such an office has the power to establish new lines. Naturally, it was hard to get to the principals of the buying office. Once seen, only the very finest of products, the ones with extraordinary promise, were taken on.

At nine in the morning I was first in line at the offices of AMC, the

American Merchandising Corporation. I was the only woman in the waiting room.

"I'd like to see Marie Weston, the cosmetics buyer, please," I ventured to the receptionist.

"She's very, very busy," was the answer. "Why don't you come back another time?"

"I don't mind waiting," I said. "Really, I don't. I'll just sit here quietly until she has a free moment."

I waited. And waited. Male salesmen for other companies were asked to come in. I waited.

"What's in your cream?" I asked a salesman who was also waiting.

"What do you mean, in it?" he asked back. "How should I know what's in it. They tell me what it is, how many ads we're going to run. They tell me it works. That's all I have to know."

I didn't answer. Inside, my mind was whirling. *My* salespeople will know what's in a product they're selling—if I ever get that far. How could he sell something so blindly? I knew what was in my cream, all right. I knew what was in every last drop of it. I could immediately tell a woman what was in it and how to use it. He was a fraud.

Still, he was called in. I waited. He came out.

"We're all going to lunch," said the brusque receptionist. "And then, Miss Weston's schedule is impossible. Really, I think you'd better come back another day. Monday would be perfect."

"Well, thank you," I said, "but I'll try waiting a little longer, as long as I'm here, if you don't mind."

Two o'clock, three o'clock, four o'clock. I waited that whole day. Feeling invisible, I was close to tears.

At five-fifteen, Miss Weston herself came out, looked at me in disbelief, and asked, "Are you still here? Well, do come in and let's have a look at what you have. Such patience must be rewarded."

It wasn't just a look at what I had that was called for at this moment. It was the experience of what I had. In two minutes, I'd opened my box of cosmetics, made up her face, then showed her how to use the back of her hand to feel the rich, softness of her "Lauder-ized" skin. She liked it—of course she did. I was lucky to find a woman buyer so that a demonstration was possible. If it were a man, I'd have demonstrated the creams anyway, but on the back of his hand. After he had noted the difference between his two hands, I would have given him some cosmetics for his wife, hoping she'd sell my product to her husband.

Miss Weston was impressed. That was the good news. The bad news was that there was still no room at any store for me.

Try us again, said Miss Weston. I'll try you again, I promised with a smile.

The smile disintegrated the moment I reached the sanctuary of home. I remember weeping that night with such despair and frustration. There was to be no rocketing into glory. Joe comforted me.

"Don't cry, honey. You got in to see her, didn't you? That was a miracle! She'll come up with a store eventually. Remember, we're in this to stay now."

He was right. I called to thank her for seeing me. I was always careful to be polite, cheerful, and generous with understanding.

Eventually, Miss Weston was able to get me a store for my line, and then Miss Mullins at another buying office found me another. I wasn't exactly riding a meteor, but the stone I was pushing was beginning to roll.

DEVOUR THE RIVAL

I researched the market and every specialty store in the country. My goal was to reach the specialty stores in the grand manner, like Saks Fifth Avenue, Bergdorf Goodman, and Bonwit Teller, where only the highest and most elegant fashions and cosmetics for women were to be found, without the distractions of housewares or furniture. There was enormous competition. The big names were Dorothy Gray, Elizabeth Arden, Germaine Monteil, and Revlon—Charles Revson's enterprise. Permit me a discreet digression on the subject of Mr. Revson.

In the cosmetics business, we have always operated according to an honor code that has turned out to be good business. The code is based quite simply on the maxim, Never knock the competition's line (at least in public). Mr. Revson subscribed to no such code when he declared himself my arch and implacable enemy from the earliest days of our competition. I'll have more to say on this subject later on, but now let it be known that since Michael Bergerac, a gentleman and a joy, took over the Revlon enterprises, things have never been the same—and to that I say thank goodness. Revson didn't let up on his attacks and his spy machinery for a moment. Once, we both happened to be at the same dinner party. Usually hostesses knew better than to seat Revson and Lauder at the same table. He curtly informed me of his intention to buy my business so that he could be the Cadillac of the cosmetics industry. I replied lightly that I thought his intention quite flattering, but that I would like to buy his business and be the Rolls Royce of the industry. Not known for his sense of humor, he stalked away without answering. War was declared. "I'll destroy her," he told some mutual friends.

People think they can eat you up and swallow you whole. The head of Fabergé, Mr. Sam Rubin, once asked me the same question: Was I for sale? He'd like to buy our business.

"You don't know much about cosmetics. Perfume is your specialty," I answered. "Why buy my business? I'll buy yours."

Something about this answer seemed to drive men wild. "Little girl," he answered in a tone that was patronizing even for those prefeminist days, "you don't know what you're talking about."

"You haven't counted what I have," I said as coldly as I could manage. "What's more, although I haven't counted what you have, I don't think you could come up with the down payment for my business."

TOUCH AND TALK, TALK AND TOUCH

In the early days, I spent an endless amount of time riding the rails. The sound of train wheels became background music to my dreams. As I traveled around the country to be present at each Estée Lauder counter opening, I met the women who would, one day, be my customers. At least I hoped they would be. To that end, I never stopped talking to people—not ever. On the way to open Auerbach's Department Store in Salt Lake City, Utah, I met the loveliest young woman in a Salvation Army dress. Lovely in spirit, that is. She was so plain in person.

Just because you're in the service of the Lord, I thought, doesn't mean you can't be beautiful. This apple-cheeked young woman's skin was as dry as the Arizona desert.

"You know, I'd love to make up your face," I told her, "and show you a cream that will make it so lovely to touch."

"Oh, no, thank you," she said, blushing. "Soap and water is just fine for my daily life."

Nonsense. I had a roomette on that train and I invited her in. A little Super-Rich All Purpose Creme, a drop of Honey Glow powder, some soft lipstick, and just a hint of turquoise eye shadow. She looked at herself—she couldn't believe it. I gave her a little of everything to take home. She still writes to me.

I talk to everyone. Once, in an elevator, a woman complimented my skin. I told her that she also had beautiful skin, but a little glow would give that skin a real lift. I just happened to have a little glow in my purse, a fresh container. I patted some on her cheeks, pressed the rest of it in her hand to take home—and made a new convert. This happened over and over and over again throughout my life. To this day I still receive mail from women I've met all over the world—met, touched, and made up during spontaneous moments.

In those early days on the road, I developed a routine that I repeated in every store where an Estée Lauder counter opened. I would be in town to make a personal appearance not just for the day, but for the week of the opening. Although my major focus was on that counter, I had work to do throughout the store. I was convinced that I could make other departments in the store work for me as they went about their own business.

I visited the sales personnel in the dress department, the hat department, the shoe department, as well as other cosmetics departments. To each saleswoman, I brought a gift of my makeup or cream, exactly what I'd be giving away to the customers as they claimed the free gifts they'd been promised in advertisements and mailings. The gift giving was not all altruistic, I must admit, although I love to make friends in this way. I knew that the women selling makeup at other counters would feel more kindly toward me if I showed them my goodwill. I was not out to take away their business, after all, but to drum up enthusiasm for my own. But, and this was more important, if I could make friends with a saleswoman selling hats, she might, just might, suggest to her customer that a free makeup at the Estée Lauder counter would enhance that new hat immeasurably. And the dress salesperson might mention to her customer that Estée Lauder has the perfect shade of lipstick to wear with the new dress.

I make the same effort today. Don't be surprised if you see a box of my gorgeous blue soaps near the beautiful blue towels in the bath department of your favorite department store, or a slip pinned to a bathing suit that reads, "Do stop by the Estée Lauder counter for a free sample of our sun cream." In the early days of my counter openings I learned the merchandising method of inducing the whole store to speak for my products.

At my own counter, I'd make up every woman who stopped to look. I would show her that a three-minute makeup could change her life. I would demonstrate that applying makeup wasn't a mystical, time-consuming process but one that should be as automatic and quick as breathing. There are those that apply makeup as if their face belongs to someone else—a kind of steely-eyed, laborious, endlessly calculating process. That's foolish at best, and at worst, ineffective. Certainly, applying makeup for a glamorous night out might take a little more time, but daytime makeup isn't an operation, isn't a life's work. It's a less-than-three-minute process.

During spare moments, I'd work the whole store. For example, I'd make a fast trip to the hat department, observe a magnificent velour hat with a gorgeous coral rose, and give the hat saleswoman a gift of a lipstick that exactly matched that rose. "When you sell the hat," I'd mention, "why don't you show your customer this lipstick and ask her to come down to the Estée Lauder counter, where she can buy the same thing?" As chance would have it, when the customer came to find the perfect lipstick for her stunning hat, she'd find many other perfect products as well.

The point was to keep thinking, keep placing the products in the public eye, keep devising new ways of capturing the consumer's attention.

During the week I usually spent at an opening promotion, I made it my business never to leave a town without seeing every beauty editor of every magazine and newspaper. I brought them samples, made up their faces, gave them beauty advice. I promoted beauty. Made friends. Everywhere, I made friends.

There is no such thing as bad times, I kept telling myself. There is no such thing as bad business. Business is there if you go after it.

And I explained everything I did, wrote instructions down on paper, prettied so many faces, touched so many faces . . .

BACK ON THE ROAD

After the first few stores, I decided to travel with a very experienced salesperson. Elizabeth Patterson helped me set up the counters, make up the women, and train the salespeople. We traveled from Dallas to Seattle, from Chicago to San Francisco. We traveled everywhere, the length and breadth of the country. In Fort Lauderdale, they called my cosmetics the Estée Lauderdale line. I didn't care what they called me as long as they were buying. In San Francisco, I waited for an hour in the rain for a taxi to take me to I. Magnin for my personal appearance in that store. I remember it clearly because I was wearing seamless stockings—unheard of at the time (I'd copied them from a model I'd seen)—my little Dior outfit of a black dress, a brown hat encrusted with tiny black beads, and cocoa-brown gloves. I always spent my money on one or two elegant outfits, which I wore everywhere, rather than on a whole wardrobe of mediocre clothes. One had to look finished to sell a fine product. Mr. Grover Magnin, the company's president, welcomed me on this particular day. He marched me up to his dress department and said to the buyer, "Look closely. This is fashion. Black with brown—daring, new, and beautiful!"

I'd also copied the black with brown motif from a model in the newest Parisian fashion magazine. With just a few good outfits, I manage to travel for weeks. Having my limited travel wardrobe cleaned from town to town and freshening up my outfits with new scarves, I'd always be immaculate. If you looked shabby or tired or messy, no one in the world would be interested in your opinion on what sells in the beauty field. You were selling yourself with each appearance, as surely as you were selling the product in your hand.

LINES OF PATTER

If they had never heard of me when I arrived in a town, they knew my name when I left. No community was too small for my attention, my absolutely full efforts. I had ridden, for instance, on a bus for six hours to open Lichtenstein's, a small store in Corpus Christi, Texas. The store's clientele was modest in size and economics. No matter. I asked the advertising department to run a newspaper advertisement that read, WHAT MAKES A CREAM WORTH $115? COME MEET ESTÉE LAUDER AND FIND OUT.

"No one here will buy a cream for that price," I was advised.

The advice didn't impress me. Never underestimate people who live in small towns or those with limited budgets. People, no matter where they live or what their finances, will spend if they're convinced of worth.

I was prepared to tell them why my cream was worth the steep price. "Why do you spend so much for a Picasso? The linen under his painting costs two dollars and seventy-five cents, each jar of paint he used was perhaps a dollar seventy-five—perhaps the material cost a total of eleven dollars. Why, then, do you pay a small fortune for a small picture? You're paying for creativity, that's why, you're paying for experience and for the ability to create something that works for you. This is the best cream in the world. It's not royal jelly with a big bunch of wax thrown in. It's a compilation of twenty-six pure ingredients. Do you know how difficult it is to get twenty-six ingredients into one magnificent cream, a cream that will make you look your loveliest at any age?"

The cream moved in a lively fashion, endearing to my heart.

There were doubters. At an opening in one town, I chaired a beauty symposium. A woman in the audience called out that she'd rather go away with her husband for a whole weekend than buy any expensive cream.

Another woman answered her for me. "Go," she said. "When you return, you'll look like an old woman from the sun. Better spend it on Estée's cream *before* you vacation."

The line was growing—and going fast. In Detroit, I walked into Himelhoch's Department Store and faced a minor disaster. There was hardly any merchandise at all left to sell, only a great deal of hand cream and lots of deep red and pale coral lipsticks. A bold step was called for.

"Well, just look at this!" I began to blend the two colors of lipstick on a customer. "If you apply the darker color over the lighter in the evening hours, you'll have the most exquisite mouth in the world. In the daylight, be sure to blend the lighter color over the deeper one. Where is it written that a woman must use only one lipstick color at a time on her mouth? Be imaginative! Be lively! Two colors give a rich, textured vibrancy that's simply magnificent. And what's more, just try this incredible hand cream on your face. If it brings such softness to your delicate hands, imagine what it can do for your facial skin."

It was all true. Two colors were divine. The cream was wonderful on the face. In one day I sold 144 tubes of hand cream and every lipstick in the store. After I left, there was an unprecedented demand for deep red and pale coral lipsticks—the two shades that were unsalable separately.

Do you want to succeed? Make the most of what you have.

COLOR NAMES

One of the reasons for our success in lipstick sales has to do with a certain accuracy in naming the colors. We've always told the consumer what to expect. When others were calling a red Love That Red, which told you nothing about the color, I was calling mine Coral Red. Coral Red, anyone could figure out, was a mix between coral and red. Flirtation Pink told the consumer that this pink was a sprightly, teasing, light pink suitable for a young woman in a white dress, for instance. A woman of fifty-five probably would not look as good in Flirtation Pink, and the very name told her so; women of fifty-five are beyond flirtation and into seduction. Rose Wood lipstick was a rosy pink with an earthy cast. Duchess Crimson immediately brought the Duchess to mind, and she always wore clear, strong reds . . . and every woman who ever read a magazine or a newspaper knew that. All Day Rose was a go-to-the-office color—nothing dramatic, just soft and pretty. Dancing Red was a go-out-in-the-evening color—bright, vivacious, exciting, dramatic. Honest, lucid, graphic descriptions—that's what I was after.

CONNECTIONS

The saleswomen were my link to the customer. "Even if no one is in the store, please don't leave your counter," I'd lecture to them. "If you're not there, the customer will not wait. You are models. You must use the cosmetics yourself, find out yourself what the best way is to apply a product. Never dip your fingers into a jar of cream and then apply your fingers to someone's face. Use a wooden spatula to invade the cream, then transfer the cream to your clean fingers. In summertime, explain that you've got a liquid diet for the face, because it's too hot for heavy creams, and demonstrate our liquid cleaner, liquid base, liquid moisturizer. In the wintertime, stress our protective super-rich creams, good to guard the face against wind and cold. Use your imagination, use your nicest manner. Tell the truth, always. Never sell what a customer doesn't want or need. Finally, if it happens to be a rainy day, and the store is quiet, call your customers on the telephone and ask them to come in for a free makeup in the newest fashion colors."

I was unstoppable, so great was my faith in what I sold. But there were moments of great heaviness in my heart. I missed my family, all those long days on the road. Career women in every age, I don't care how powerful and effective they are, will always have the problem of juggling priorities. It's not easy, but take heart, it's possible to handle many things at once. My family has always taken precedence over all other things, but I have never felt the need to choose between family and business. I could, I would, I have both. Perhaps I missed some small part of my sons' growing up, perhaps I was not there at one or two crucial moments, but I was building something for all of us. I called home every night. I kept in constant touch when I was on the road. I even called my own parents almost every night to allay their worries. You're never too grown-up to stop being a child to your parents. In each of us is the seed of the child we were and the adult we will become. To our parents, the differences are blurred.

It was an enormous solace to know that Joe was home with the boys every night. We had an excellent housekeeper as well—not excellent enough ever to really satisfy me—but the best alternative to me I could find. Today, so many women are searching for the same alternative as they juggle home and career. I wish them well!

On the road I never allowed myself to feel complacent. There was always a little more cream to sell after you sold the last lipstick. I set monetary goals for each day and urged the women behind my counters to set such standards for themselves. A dramatic instance of my goal-oriented behavior occurred one day in Houston. I have to laugh myself as I recall it. The store was Sakowitz, the closing minutes were almost upon us, and I had slipped off my shoes to count up the day's sales. I was aiming for a thousand dollars.

Oh, no. Nine hundred and ninety-eight dollars. Spotting a customer making it through the door just as it was closing on her heels, I nearly tripped as I stepped back into my shoes and stopped her mid-dash.

"Madam, I have something that would be just wonderful for you. May I take a second to show it to you?"

"No—no—I'm in a huge hurry," she answered.

"But, madam," I continued, "I have an eye cream that will help smooth out those little wrinkles around your eyes, and the ones on the side of your mouth."

That did it. She stopped dead in her tracks. "What do you mean, on the side of my mouth?"

"Those tiny little lines, right there, just like the ones around the eyes. The cream is only two dollars and ninety-five cents a jar. I have one left. You really should have it."

She rummaged in her purse, found the money, took the jar, and rushed away.

Letting my shoes drop off, I sank into my chair and grinned my most victorious grin. I knew the cream would be splendid for her lines and I'd made my thousand, plus gained another faithful customer, I was sure.

Recently I had occasion to meet Mr. Robert Sakowitz, now the store president, who told me he'd never forgotten the day when he, as a young boy working for his father, saw me slip off my shoes—and get them back on in a matter of three seconds flat.

I'd take even less time today. It wasn't youth that made me so energetic, it was enthusiasm. That's why I know a woman of any age has it within her to begin a business or a life's work of any sort. It's a fresh outlook that makes youth so attractive anyway, that quality of anything's possible. That spirit is not owned only by those under thirty. Selling, especially, is an art form that depends on spirit—and honesty. The customer can always tell when you're being less than candid. I once heard a customer ask my salesgirl if the lipstick she was about to purchase would come off when she ate.

"Oh, no," replied the well-meaning salesgirl. "It's really almost indelible—"

"Madam," I interjected with a smile, "if it never came off, I'd be out of business."

EARLY NETWORKING

While I was traveling, Joe had begun to work with a brilliant young chemist from International Flavors and Fragrances. Together they would pore over creams and formulas to find new, safe ways of producing natural beauty. Dr. Jerry Amsterdam paved the way for the hundreds of chemists who eventually worked for our company, but in the early days it was just Joe and he, with my help, who mixed, tested, discarded, and discovered the ingredients that were to be the hallmarks of excellence and purity.

Our roles, by this time, were quite clear. Joe ran the factory and dealt with numbers and production. I ran the sales force. Leonard, still a teenager, ran errands during the weekend: mailing packages to stores, delivering samples to buyers—getting the feel of the business. Ronald, still a young child, drank in the activity of his very busy family. There was no such thing as Saturday or Sunday in my life, neither on the road, when I used every second to make friends and to spread the word about our products, nor at home, when I'd often work at my desk until I saw the light creeping into the window and realize I'd have just a couple of hours of sleep until it was time to begin another day.

And, then, there were good friends. How much do I owe to the electric, always-thinking presence of Helen Blake? She had a genius— and it's my good fortune to have recognized that in her—of spotting possibility. For a time, she worked for Mary Chess and then for Lanvin. We came to like and respect each other. She was, is, my friend. Never underestimate the value of an ally.

"You know," she would say to me quite casually during a phone call, "I think you might give Miss Bea Pope, the merchandise manager from Woodward and Lothrop, a call. I was with her yesterday, and she mentioned that I looked wonderful. I told her it was due to your cosmetics, and, well, I just think she'd like to know more about you."

That instant I'd call Miss Pope. (If you don't do important things when you think of them, you probably never will and may lose out.)

Then Helen Blake would say, "I was thinking about Marshall Field's buyer, Harold Bierbaum. He's quite difficult to get to see, but I believe he'd be worth the effort."

That instant I'd call Mr. Bierbaum.

Today they call it networking—this sharing between colleagues. It is one of the most powerful tools in the business. First, you learn to ask the right questions. Next, you learn to listen to answers. Even oblique answers. Then, you learn to act without weeks of deep introspection, without weeks of self-questioning. You move. You pick up the telephone or you take the train to the place where your interests lie. Your friend has helped you to get there. In business, as in human relations, it's that rare touch, that person-to-person contact, that leaves the deepest impression. If you try to impress someone with your power or your wisdom, you will find it hard going. If you are sensitive to his needs, to what will bring him happiness, talking to him of his daughter's school or of the island he and his wife have discovered, you will make him your friend. Moreover, if you treat this new friend with dignity and

My sister Renee read when I wasn't brushing her hair.

Renee and I—
with nautical flair.

Developing my ''nose''—
at thirteen—in a field of
fragrance.

Renee and I on a swing, watching the world go by.

Graduation Day at P.S. 14; I'm on the right, sheltering a friend beneath my mother's silver-handled umbrella.

In those days, the license came with the car. Renee and I, out for a spin.

My mother and father, in their
eighties, at his cemetery property. Today, an airplane view
would reveal the oval trotting
track where we rode our
ponies.

My father, Max Mentzer, and
one of his trotters.

At home in Corona, Queens.

Joe (in knickers) and his
"Blondie." We were engaged.

True love.

Our honeymoon trip to Bermuda,
on the ship *Bermudiana*.

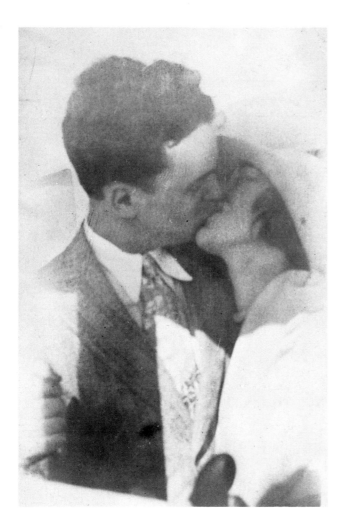

◀ The bride's face was glowing. Estée Lauder
made the New York *Times* rotogravure for the
first time.

The smiling product of the House of Ash Blondes.

The Vamp. I may not have endured as an actress, but my talent for the dramatic has survived intact.

Joe kept his promise, and we moved to
New York City.

The future Chief Executive Officer,
Leonard Lauder, and his proud mother.

A salesperson has to sell herself as much as her product. I always wore the best and I was rarely without a hat. I still have the sequined blouse.

One of our very first orders to Philadelphia. Prices have gone up since then.

This is my first formal publicity portrait—the original Estée Lauder.

Personal appearances
always brought throngs
of women, all asking for
advice. I touched
many faces.

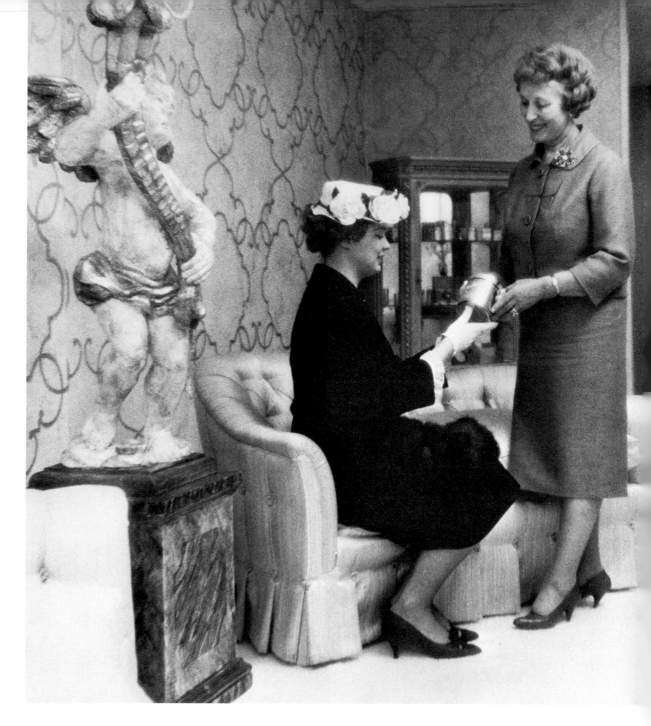

"Please let me show you why your store's customers will just love Renutriv—even at a hundred and twenty five dollars a jar." At our first showroom, 666 Fifth Avenue, I had to convince every buyer to take a chance on me.

Joe and I celebrated Elizabeth Patterson's birthday at the Stork Club. She was my traveling assistant for many years.

Irwin Dribben

Lunching at the Stork Club with Miss Sally McCoy, cosmetics buyer for R. H. Stearns in Boston, and two saleswomen who were visiting New York for the first time.

I was happiest with Ronald and Leonard. ''You get out of children what you put in,'' Joe always said.

The family arrives for a Florida vacation. Every possible spare moment away from business was spent together.

respect, offer him your warmth and hospitality, you will also have an ally, as I had in Helen Blake.

Imagine a business world where you are the seller and the buyers are your allies.

Then, make it happen. Here is how I made it happen.

At 15 East Fifty-third Street, I had a little office and an even smaller terrace, a very tiny terrace. If you lived next door and observed the happenings on that terrace during a few weeks of every year, you'd have thought that the luncheons you saw served were of a purely social nature. You'd be wrong. It always seemed to me that limiting business to a sterile atmosphere, behind desks with office chairs and business frames of mind, was a mistake. I was a woman, and my natural habitat was a lovely home with the most gracious of furnishings. It seemed obvious from the start that I should use my womanness as an asset rather than a liability, and so I established my own version of today's business lunch. Instead of two martinis, I offered a fine wine. Instead of restaurant silver, I served with my own precious sterling, my finest dishes. Instinct told me to entertain buyers as I would my dearest friends, making no concessions to the brusque business manners my competitors employed. It was not in an office I'd meet the buyers who were from out of town, it was within the ambience of that tiny terrace, which was just big enough to accommodate a beautiful white wrought-iron table and six matching chairs. I had a cheerful blue and white awning constructed for intimacy and protection, and I covered the terrace floor with an artificial grass rug.

My secret weapon happened to be next door. It was called the Stork Club. Certainly, it would have been possible to escort the buyers to the Stork Club itself, where Sherman Billingsly, the man who prided himself on exclusivity, would have played host, but it was I who wished to be hostess. I wanted to project the image of home. Still, it was the Stork Club that catered the beautiful salads, the elegant desserts, the impressive wines. Three or four times a week, when the buyers came to New

York, Billingsly's white-gloved waiters would arrive to serve the prettiest lunch imaginable on my terrace, with my linens. If an out of town buyer wished to visit the renowned Stork Club, we'd dine there.

It was, if I do say so myself, an inspired, festive success. All week the buyers had been barraged with competitors' sales campaigns in formal restaurants and formal offices. On the terrace of my office they were treated to a friendly repast—spirited, elegant, personal. They relaxed, and so did I. We chatted and laughed and came to know one another as people because no business at all was discussed during lunch. I believe buyers look forward to a tranquil lull in a sea of hard-sell crusades. Homes, families, and good-natured gossip were the order of the afternoon. The knack of bringing humanity to one's business is the greatest asset of any business person.

After lunch, I went to work. I, not they. Each female buyer was treated to a makeup while the others watched, laughed, and commented. Each male buyer saw the products demonstrated on the back of his hand. Everyone was given samples to take home to friends and wives. The women buyers, in particular, were eager for news of the market—what was new, what would work on them and the customers. I was happy to personalize.

Then, we talked tactics. We'd sit down to arrange a year's itinerary of promotions, introductions of new products, and newspaper advertisements.

CHAMPION GIVEAWAYS

I made my own suggestions for the promotion-minded stores. Since I pioneered the giveaway promotion, I had specific thoughts about its best uses. A truism was becoming increasingly apparent: cream, even the most stellar cream in the world, wouldn't draw a woman to the store. Your giveaway simply couldn't be cream alone. No one would stand in a line, fight a crowd, or brave the rain or a crowded department store to get a free gift of a skin-treatment product. I suppose customers reasoned that skin care was essential but not a fast route to glamour, and glamour was the irresistible draw. Powder and glow were enticing, we discovered, but not irresistible. Which cosmetic was the best of all, the item that would entice a customer to come, receive, and then buy more? Lipstick, always lipstick. A woman would walk a mile for a brilliant, new lipstick color. The rule that emerged, as I explained to the buyers, is that color is essential in giveaway promotions. Today, when you receive our mailings that offer you Gifts With Purchase, you will note that a lipstick is always among the gifts. Later, we saw fragrance as the next best giveaway; it was never as strong as a lipstick, but powerful as a combination—color and fragrance—that seemed to hit all bases. The buyers were grateful for such insights. We all enjoyed our afternoon. Need I mention that the forthcoming orders were heart-warming?

Most important, we'd make contact, the human variety. I felt I knew who was buying; they felt they knew who was selling. We all knew more about each other than when we first started thinking about doing business together.

This was an important concept. Generosity is met with generosity. It's a business tactic as well as a rule of human kindness. Take the case of the metal lipsticks. The chairperson (in those days she was known as the chairman) of an important charity came to me with a request: "We're having the biggest luncheon to raise money in our chapter's history. We desperately need a gift for all the ladies."

Obviously, the only gift every woman would love would be a lipstick. But there was a problem. The war was on. Metal was as scarce as hens' teeth. The only lipsticks I had were in metal cases, and I had been saving them.

There was no alternative. I couldn't turn down an outstretched hand. I never could. There were eighty-two women invited to that luncheon and I gave eighty-two lipsticks to the chairperson to use as gifts at the table.

My theory held true. Whatever you give comes back to you. Every one of those eighty-two women belonged to three other organizations. Every one of those eighty-two women must have talked about the marvelous new lipsticks, because word spread. We sold and sold and sold. Even today, I'll occasionally meet a woman who'd heard about the wonderful metal lipsticks at the luncheon so many years ago.

That was the first time I'd ever donated gifts for a charity affair, but, I can assure you, I've been donating ever since. Of course, there are people who ask for help who don't really need it. How do you know who deserves your charity and who does not? You never really do. That's why you must give to everyone so that you don't inadvertently turn down the outstretched hand that's really needy.

Those who have must always give to others. Even those who don't have should give what they can. What you give comes back.

So we gave to each other, the buyers and I at the tiny office at 15 East Fifty-third Street. What we gave was friendship. Let me tell you a bit about that office.

AMBIENCE IS ALL

It looked as if a woman lived there, a woman who cared about grace and style. There would be no point in decorating an environment for selling beauty in a heavy leather-chair, early-attorney style. I opted for presentation. Decorating with the precision of a diamond cutter, I chose Victorian furniture, deep-pile deep-blue carpets, fragile Chinese vases, and hand-painted rice paper. My very first office was elegant, although it consisted of two small offices and a reception area. I had the walls mirrored, so that by the time I put a desk in one corner and feminine rich fabrics throughout, the two rooms looked like four. If I had to spend time in a tiny office, it was going to please my eye, not the eye of a decorator who had fixed ideas of what an office should look like.

In our offices today, high in the General Motors building in New York, you'll see the original sofa, recovered (I waste nothing good). The view is literally dizzying. The city lies below in all its bustle, fervor, beauty, energy.

Shades of Lauder blue are everywhere. Porcelain bowls of French beaded flowers, porcelain birds of jeweled hues, drapes copied from the Schönbrunn Palace in Vienna, glittering crystal, antique gilt furniture, Oriental carpets resting on Lauder blue carpeting, a private dining room . . . We've spun gold from the purest of creams and fragrances! It's very thrilling.

But I loved that tiny office just as much.

Make the most of what you have. I operated, full time, on that precept. If you can't have everything you think you deserve at that moment, you would do well to surround yourself with symbols of your ideals. In that small office, I surrounded myself with touches of the good life, the lovely and intricately tapestried life of my imagination, an imagination that has always been, I'm proud to say, large enough to admit any possibility.

We didn't stay in those offices very long. Eventually, we moved to the Tishman Building at 666 Fifth Avenue. Femininity got us there, not male power.

I was taking a trip to Europe, on the *Queen Elizabeth,* to scout out the market. One evening at dinner on this lovely ship, a gentleman at my table asked me to dance.

"My name is David Tishman," he said during the waltz, "and you have beautiful skin."

How could I *not* have beautiful skin? I thought.

"Tishman, Tishman . . . Are you in the dress business?" I asked sweetly.

"No, I'm not in the dress business. I'm a real estate owner, the biggest in New York, maybe in the country." He seemed a bit annoyed.

I knew that name sounded familiar.

I was my most charming self that evening. You wouldn't know that a salesman of the first order lurked beneath that charm. I don't think

Mr. Tishman actually got over the fact that his name meant so little to me at the time. When I returned home after the trip, there was a message waiting for me from his office.

Let me make a long story short: we moved into the Tishman Building at a very favorable rent. Mr. Tishman's kindness served to impress upon me how very important a gentleman he was and how very important retaining my femininity was—especially aboard ship.

THE EGG AND I

Sometimes, iconography is thrust upon one by circumstances rather than by choice. I am sure I never thought much about eggs, nor would I have chosen an egg to be a symbol of permanent, personal significance, but an egg it turned out to be. An egg, of all things, was an absolutely perfect symbol of the products to which I'd devoted my life.

Consider the egg. It is fluid and pure. It's a haven for new life, for youth. It symbolizes rebirth, freshness, newness. It is, perhaps, perfect in design and has all it needs to function in its clean, durable, spare form. It is fragile, yet solidly nourishing. It is nurturing. An egg is close to divine.

My mother used to put beaten whole egg on her face as a masque, and she'd also use an egg in her hair when she rinsed it to give it luster. Eggs had restorative properties, no doubt about it. We spoke to our chief chemist, Dr. Jerry Amsterdam, and asked him to come up with a face cream that would be made from the whole egg, that would be the finest cream ever produced.

Estoderme Youth-Dew Creme was the result. We knew it was unique, and we had high hopes for its success. Part of its success depended on magazine approval. A new service had arrived in America. The best women's magazines had installed trustworthy laboratories in their offices, where they would test the products being advertised in the nation's press. Were the products what they said they were? If a product was said to contain vitamins, did it? Women were coming to rely on this service. *Harper's Bazaar* set up a laboratory with particularly stringent testing. A lot depended on winning its seal of approval.

Miss Sara Lee was the beauty editor at *Harper's*. One day, she called to ask if Carmel Snow, *Harper's* editor in chief, could stop by to meet me. Carmel Snow was a legend. She knew the "beautiful people" of the world, hobnobbed with the rich, the famous, and the intellectual, used Paris and Switzerland as a playground and testing ground. She also had enormous power. If she liked you, Carmel Snow could make you. If she found you to be a fraud, she could break you—no questions asked. She had fantastic glamour. She arrived in a hot pink Balenciaga suit and a beautiful hat to match—just my kind of style. She imperiously took a seat opposite me to hear about my cosmetics. Hear about them? That wasn't my style.

When I took out the Estoderme and applied it to Miss Snow's face inside of thirty seconds, Sara Lee turned gray. Later she told me that, just as with a drowning man, images of her nice life at the magazine kept floating in front of her bearing a legend, "This is it, Sara, you're fired."

Indeed, Miss Snow did look astonished.

But I kept going; speed was on my side. In another second, I had wiped off the cream, put on some glow, a touch of our newest lipstick, a little powder. In no time, she was finished. From her expression, it was clear that Sara Lee also thought *she* was finished.

"Your skin is very fragile," I told Miss Snow. "This will help you to preserve it. It's Estoderme Creme, made of the whole egg . . . absorbed into the skin . . . will nourish you inside as well as out . . . it's just lovely . . . so now are you."

I think that most people were afraid to look at Carmel Snow, let alone touch her face. I put her hand to her face, let her feel the new texture of her skin. Showed her a mirror.

"My dear," she finally said. "I never expected, I never thought, you would do . . . that. But yes, actually, it's quite nice."

She set her laboratories to work. The inspectors tested. They found vitamins, softening agents, and pure egg. Of course they did.

In October 1951 *Harper's Bazaar* ran a picture of two, small perfect eggs, enhanced by their own shadows and their singular purity. No pictures of cosmetics. No models. Just the two eggs.

"The egg and Estée Lauder" ran the caption, and then, "Estée Lauder's clients have long claimed that her creams were 'good enough to eat' besides being immeasurably good for complexions. Her latest cream is a genuine innovation—included in its formula is the whole egg, reinforced with ingredients which act on the skin like hormones, but which are not. Its effect—a lovely dewy freshness; and in time an effective blandishment against wrinkles. A soft, unquestionably beautifying cream. Estoderme Youth Dew, $6.50 plus tax." (Alas, like everything else, the price has risen.)

Estoderme, unlike my Creme Pack, also smelled wonderful. The sweet smell of success—it's intoxicating.

CHAPTER 4

YOUTH DEW AND BEYOND

I never knew I was a "nose." It took until 1953 to find out what being a nose really meant.

In Gertrude Stein's world, a nose is a nose is a nose, but in the world of perfume, a nose is a rare person, one who possesses a special olfactory sense and who can identify exactly what components make up a fragrance (a little of this, a lot of that, a minuscule dash of that). A nose can differentiate between a great and irresistible scent and a mediocre one. The greatest perfumers in the world have all been noses.

Once, in Paris, several years ago, Ernest Shifton, chief perfumer of International Flavors and Fragrances, the company responsible for many of the finest essences in perfumery, announced at a conference of international perfumers, "In all America, there is only one true nose and it belongs to Estée Lauder."

A gallant, Gallic toast indeed, especially when one considers the chauvinistic attitude of the traditional French world of excellent perfumes. Well, then, so be it: I was a nose.

But I didn't know it in 1953. All I knew was that I couldn't stand seeing all those bottles of perfume, gathering dust, evaporating, being saved for occasions and resting unused on the elegant dressers of my friends. Bottles of perfumes were displayed so proudly—unopened. Why didn't women use their perfume? I wondered. Why did it take a special occasion to open a bottle of scent? Most perfumes, I knew, would evaporate down to an unpleasantly pungent base while waiting to be used on these rare occasions.

I knew what the trouble was. Perfume was the perfect gift. *That* was killing it.

Only a rare woman would walk into a department store and buy perfume for herself. Traditionally, women in America were passive about smelling wonderful. It was proper to wait for your loved one to present you with a bottle of something he liked, or something that he thought you might like. And if you had no such loved one? It was unthinkable, self-indulgent, narcissistic, and even decadent to treat yourself to fragrance. Oh, you could buy an inexpensive bottle of cologne. Nothing more significant.

What nonsense. I'd always chosen my own scent and I always made myself responsible for having a quantity of it on hand.

One evening, at a dinner party, staring at one more dresser tray with three unopened pretty bottles of perfume, I had an idea. I'd convince the American woman to buy her own perfume, as she would buy a lipstick.

Simple? Yes. Just like Gift With Purchase. Too simple for anyone to bother with.

There was a scent I'd been exposed to for years. My uncle had created it for a Russian princess and my mother always had it around the house. It wasn't exactly right, though . . . not exactly. For months, I worked on it. I bought essences and dozens of tiny bottles. I experimented and experimented until I found a scent that pleased me enormously. It was sweet, it was warm, it was diffusive, that is, it would easily intermingle with flesh and with water. The last was essential to my idea.

How could I get the American woman to buy her own perfume? *I would not call it perfume.* I would call it Youth Dew. A *bath oil* that doubled as a skin perfume. That would be acceptable to buy because it was feminine, all-American, very girl-next-door to take baths, wasn't it? A woman could buy herself a bottle of bath oil the way she'd buy a lipstick—without feeling guilty, without waiting for her birthday, anniversary, graduation, without giving tiresome hints to her husband. I believe that advances for women got a boost when a woman felt free to dole out some of her own dollars for her own choice of scents.

I had another idea. I wouldn't seal the cap of the Youth Dew bottle as the French perfumers did. Why should I make my creation inaccessible? If the bottle were unsealed, a browsing customer could unscrew the cap (as every customer secretly wishes to do), take a whiff, and by the time that occurred, she'd have the essence on her hands. Now, the customer might well leave my counter, but she'd be smelling Youth Dew wherever she went. Chances were excellent that she'd return to the source, the scent leading the way, and buy that source for her very own.

To this day, I never burden my fragrances with superfluous layers of sealed cellophane or tight, impossible-to-unwind twists of gold wire to make opening and using the fragrance a chore. The gold wire we use is purely decorative: it's not there to guard the bottle against an experimental whiff.

The bath oil that doubled as a perfume took the cosmetics industry by storm. Women responded with delight, unhesitatingly bought then poured the precious liquid into their bath water, and reveled in sweetened auras for hours and hours afterward. We were inundated by letters. One woman wrote me that her husband was bored. I answered her, ''Put a little Youth Dew in your bath and you'll see how bored he is.'' To this day she credits me with saving her marriage. I'm confident she's correct.

Youth Dew did have romantic undertones, but some were not quite so positive. Let me tell you about the Angry Man. When the perfume was launched, we were among the first to have the store send little blotters saturated with the scent along with customers' bills. It was tremendously effective. You'd open your monthly statement and get hit with a delightful fragrance along with the bill. Blotters worked splendidly—until the Angry Man.

He'd collected his bills at his office and stuffed them into his suit pocket as he left for home. When he arrived, he was a walking garden of a husband, an aura of Youth Dew wafting from his pocket. An enraged wife accused him of serious wrongdoing.

The Angry Man wrote an angry letter to Mr. Walter Hoving, then the president of Bonwit Teller, and Mr. Hoving ruled there would be no more blotters unless they were enclosed in something to conceal the scent until the customer *wanted* to smell like a garden.

That's why, in case you have ever wondered, perfume blotters come sealed in tiny glassine envelopes when they're enclosed in your bill. Today, scents are sometimes implanted along the gummed seal of a crease of paper. The fragrance is released only when a customer opens the seal. The Angry Man doesn't know it, but he changed merchandising in a very substantial way.

THE SWEET SMELL OF SUCCESS

What was especially wonderful about the new bath oil was that it lasted and lasted. It wasn't tentative and frightened, as many scents are. Not only were the oils rich, but the new process we developed which released molecules of fragrance on the body sporadically rather than all at once. It was a breakthrough. No longer did women have to douse themselves with scent in the morning, only to have it evaporate by the time they reached their destination. Youth Dew lasted. We created a mini revolution, and the whole world, as I saw it, took on a fresher, more stimulating aspect. Instead of using their French perfumes by the drop, behind each ear, women were using Youth Dew by the bottle in their bath water.

It doesn't take a graduate of business school to figure out that meant sales, beautiful sales, for Joe and me. In 1953 Youth Dew did about $50,000 worth of business for us. In 1984 that figure had jumped to over a $150 million dollars.

When Youth Dew was born, an executive at Neiman-Marcus in Dallas took me out to dinner while visiting New York. I patted a few drops of Youth Dew on his hand to let him experience the new fragrance his store would soon be selling. The next day, he confessed he hadn't closed his eyes. Titillating visions of a beautiful, fragrant woman sleeping beside him kept him awake all night.

Dolores Del Rio announced in public that the secret to "driving men ga-ga" was wearing one's hair in an upsweep that has been brushed with Youth Dew. "The way you smell," said one "ga-ga" gentleman, trembling, to her, she reported, "I'll never let you go."

Upsweeps brushed with Youth Dew were seen in the best places.

A man named Ralph Lindo came along from Panama, and I wanted very much to sell him on being our distributor there. I picked up some Youth Dew and said, "Here, smell this." And what do you know—I accidentally spilled some on him. Well, he washed and he rubbed and he couldn't get that fragrance off. The tenacity of Youth Dew actually convinced him. And he's still with our company!

Joan Crawford once gave an interview in which she said that she'd enticed her husband Alfred Steele by dabbing a bit of Youth Dew in her hair. "I can't stop dancing with you," said Mr. Pepsi-Cola, "you smell so exquisite."

We were a hit. The nose knew we were in business.

I think the legendary Chanel put it best. "Perfume," she said, "is the unseen but unforgettable and ultimate fashion accessory. It heralds a woman's arrival and prolongs her departure."

Perfume was in our lives.

A recent New York *Times* article literally equated scents with success, claiming that fragrances have been associated with images of success and power historically and currently. A 1984 survey compiled for the Fragrance Foundation queried 486 women executives on their fragrance habits; more than half said they wore perfume every workday, and 88 percent said they used it at least once a week. An additional 36 percent said they believed wearing a fragrance to work helped a woman's career! One woman questioned for the *Times* article said that fragrance gave her more of a lift than a new dress. "The dress comes off, but the fragrance stays on."

When I began in the industry, fragrance was a luxury, not a tool for success. I am proud to think that I had something to do with encouraging the American woman to wear perfume every day of the week.

I knew I had to develop my nose further. It was fifteen years before I felt the next scent was ready to be brought out, but it took fifteen years to come to understand the nuances and possibilities of this extraordinary fragrance.

As I worked, I realized that I literally was able to see fragrance as well as smell it . . . and that's no exaggeration. Couldn't everyone? Apparently not. So palpable a presence was a beautiful scent that I could see a splendid aura around the woman who wore it. Sometimes the perfume would have faint color to my eye, sometimes it would almost vibrate in ethereal waves. Perfume had a perceptible presence. When a woman dabs a drop of a fine scent on her body, the aura and she become one. It seemed to me that a woman wearing a magnificent scent became lush and desirable right before my eyes. I have watched innumerable husbands and lovers respond to scent in the most amazing ways. It's gratifying to see.

MYTHS AND MISTAKES

As I read and experimented, I came to question the existing myths about fragrances.

Apply it skimpily on little pulse points? Wrong. That's for the old-fashioned woman, the woman who is "saving" her perfume, the woman who shuns self-indulgence. The best way to apply fragrance, I discovered and taught my customers, is to spray it into the air in front of you and to walk into it. Wearing perfume is like loving. You can't be stingy. You have to give yourself abundantly, not a little here and there. I knew there was more to perfume than a pretty scent; there has to be an idea behind it. Fragrance exists in the mind, not just in the nose.

Another myth suggested that women choose a fragrance and wear it day and night. It would become her signature. But fragrance, I knew, was much more than a signature; it was a whole personality! Women often have one personality in the day and another in the romantic evening hours. Why not have a rich and varied perfume wardrobe? If fragrances were compatible, it would be possible. I knew it was old-fashioned to stick to one scent. If fragrances did not fight one another, did a woman have to pledge eternal allegiance to just one? I changed my clothes between the time I awoke and the time I went to sleep. Why should I not change my fragrance as well to fit my mood and destination? The key word was compatible. No fragrance should be overpowering—that was the only sensible rule. If a woman's perfume preceded her entrance and didn't arrive with her, she was wearing too much or the wrong perfume. But a perfume in the morning and a different one in the afternoon and yet another fragrance in the evening—yes, it would work!

Yet another myth persisted, namely, that two perfumes couldn't be blended. More nonsense. All one had to do was look at a hill fragrant and ablaze with a thousand different blooms to see that pure scents didn't clash with one another. Surely you could apply one scent while another precious scent still lingered.

I was absolutely determined to provide my customers with a rich and textured choice of scents—interchangeable, adaptable, exquisite.

The myths had to go.

THE TEST OF TRUTH

It was time to develop a testing routine if I was to make a life's work of creating great new perfumes. I knew how complicated the testing procedures of the great noses in Europe were, but I didn't need such pomp and ceremony. The method I devised was basic and simple. It took time—years and years of trial in some cases—but it never fails to work.

When I'm testing a new scent, I'll mix dozens and dozens of precious oils until I have a possibility that pleases me enormously. I wear the new fragrance day and night. I wear it to sleep and to the office and out to dinner. Successful fragrances must stir the emotions. If a scent is truly great, people love it instantly. If it's not great, they'll hate it instantly. Rarely is there an in-between reaction. It's either "Fantastic!" or "Impossible!"

If you are within arm's reach of me, and I am testing a new fragrance, I'll rub a generous amount, not a skimpy drop, inside your palm and ask how you like it. The truth is, I won't pay too much attention to your answer. I'll watch your eyes. If they come alive with pleasure, it's a yes. Certainly, if I rub some perfume on your hand, politeness will take hold of you, and even if you hate it, you'll murmur, "Mmmm, yes, it's lovely," but your eyes won't lie. If they stay dull, if they don't dance with wonder, back to a new vial I'll go. I ask elevator operators, taxi drivers, society women, princes, professors, "Do you like this? Would your wife like it?" And their eyes answer.

Youth Dew seized on the American woman's new interest in body care, something European women discovered centuries ago. In Paris, a woman would buy a body cream even faster than she would a face cream. Actually, I had gone back to my roots; the mineral baths my mother enjoyed were not the whim of one woman but a passion of generations of women.

Estée was born next.

I'm quite serious when I say that I *see* a fragrance. Once at a party after Youth Dew came out, I saw the light from two crystal chandeliers shimmering in a glass of champagne. Imagine if I could capture that image in a fragrance, I immediately thought. For years I worked on that incredible light.

I mixed hundreds of precious essences in every possible combination until, one day, I had what I searched for—the light in the champagne. Five hundred or so experimental "Estée possibles" were discarded and only one, the final choice, remained. It was young, exciting, sensual. The day sensual goes out of business, so will Estée Lauder. But my kind of sensuality is not blatant or harsh. It is seductive and suggestive. Think of a glass parson's table on a white fur rug. Sleek, cool, sophisticated. Think of velvety voices. Think of light in champagne.

Why did I name this new scent after myself—this of all scents? I didn't. It named itself. I would give out samples to the women in my office to try, and friends asked them, "What are you wearing?"

"It's Estée's perfume," was the answer. Estée it became.

To tell you the truth, I loved the idea of a gorgeous fragrance bearing my name. Now, that's immortality. Pat Buckley was wearing Estée when Nancy Reagan came to visit. Nancy admired the fragrance, and Pat promptly gave Mrs. Reagan her own bottle. Mrs. Luz Patino, the Brazilian platinum king's wife, is also a fan. I like knowing that Estée is present at places that are a long way from Corona.

Azurée was the next fragrance. It was a tangy, citrusy scent, a pretty perfume that conjured up images of a golden girl basking languorously on a Mediterranean beach. At least that's what *I* envisioned when I smelled Azurée.

Business was going well. I thought I could focus on our business without outside distractions, but I was naïve. There was a new worry at hand.

SPIES

The spy network was awesome.

All I wanted—and you'll have to believe that I'm being honest—was to be left alone to do my work. It became evident that secrecy in the development of our products was required because our competitors spent more time trying to "scoop" our new ideas than developing new ideas of their own. Sometimes they were less than inspired in their spy tactics. A young man applied to my husband for a factory position and was told that no jobs were available at the moment. "I'll work for nothing," he answered earnestly. "I'd just love to work for you so much, you don't even have to pay me."

Really, young man, we thought. How altruistic. Did he believe for one moment we didn't realize he was here to watch and copy?

We began an elaborate coding system. Test fragrances would never have ingredients specified on vials, but would, instead, have numbers or letters that made sense to only me, Joe, or our sons. If an interested party happened to get his hands on a fragrance under consideration in our perfumery, he'd read that the vial he stole was none other that 007 or ZHR13 or BFXZ. That information couldn't help him much.

We operate today in the same fashion. After I've finally found exactly the right fragrance for which I have been searching, I give the formula to our perfumery, which will then make up the large quantities of perfume that will be shipped to stores. But I never give the whole formula. When the mixture is 95 percent or even 98 percent completed and the great vats of perfume are ready to be bottled, one member of the Lauder family goes to the factory to supply the missing secret 5 or 2 percent, the ingredient without which the fragrance can never be complete. No one can ever copy us. That final ingredient is never known to our factories, essence suppliers, anyone. Only a Lauder knows it.

Still, they try. In particular, Mr. Revson tried to market our ideas. Sophisticated spying equipment was Charles's specialty. We had friends who told us that his instruments alone were awesome, let alone the technology required to run them. I heard he had a spectroscope to analyze the colors in competitors' products in his Bronx laboratory. He had an infrared version, an atomic absorption spectroscope, and an ultraviolet spectroscope. He would not only have our colors analyzed, but fragrances and containers as well. In fact, he copied us so much that I must admit when he died, something was lost in our business, some subtle enjoyment, some jolting of complacency. It's irritating to have competitors hot on your heels, but it's also flattering and stimulating.

Let me give you an example of Revson's machinery. I launched Estée; he came out with Charlie. We decided to use a single model exclusively—Karen Graham; he decided to try the same thing with Lauren Hutton. After Gift With Purchase hit the market from our counters, Revlon also offered Gift With Purchase.

Clinique, which I'll cover in detail later, was a scientific breakthrough. Hot on the heels of Clinique was Mr. Revson's Etherea—same concept but different quality. With Aramis, I was the first to launch men's skin care products, with fashion cachet and clout as well as quality; he was just behind with Braggi. We had a very dark, brown box; he made a very dark brown box. We lined our box with brown; so did he, but, a white edge peeked out of his box. He had his people sitting in his factory for weeks, handpainting the edges of his boxes brown.

I wasn't worried; his products could never measure up to ours. The only problem was the possibility that the consumer would confuse our original with his copy and the real thing would be tarnished in comparison.

I retaliated on only one occasion just to let Mr. Revson know that we were quite aware of his "interest" in our products and that we were quite capable of finding out the secrets of others—if we wanted to go that route. Inside information told us that Etherea was going to try to give Clinique a run for its money. Advertising was not our favored method of spreading the word, but on this occasion, we took out ads for Clinique in *Women's Wear Daily*. In the ads, we used phrases that were admittedly Revson's own phrases from his Etherea campaign, which would be running soon. Phrases like "personal skin index" and "biologically correct" were sprinkled throughout our copy. Our purpose was to send a message to Revson saying, "Two can play at the same game so be careful." In addition, integrated with the copy of our advertisements were many phrases and words taken directly from a secret memo Mr. Revson had issued to his top people. We wanted him to understand that we could reciprocate if we were pushed too far.

"HIM"

This strategy was not true to my nature though. I didn't thrive on fighting. If Elizabeth Arden's claim to fame was pink, and Revlon's was sexiness and nail enamel, mine was, I hoped, elegance. I much preferred to remove myself from the fray, remain a lady at all costs, stay out of the scandal limelight, and stick to my business, not anyone else's.

This was, of course, most especially true when Revson was very big and we were still very small. The less we had to do with the Nail Man, as Helena Rubinstein dubbed him, the better off I thought we'd be. I didn't want to spark his interest, his competitive spirit, his need to copy. I tried to keep a low profile and stay out of his sphere. When Leonard first came into our business, he wasn't sure he agreed with this stance. Revlon was very strongly committed to nail enamel. We were not. One day, Leonard came into my office—I was still his boss then.

"I think we should make nail polish," he said. "We've been getting a lot of calls for it."

I remember my response. "I don't want to get started with him," I said.

"I don't know who 'him' is, and I really want to go in and start selling nail lacquers," said Leonard.

"I am not getting started with him," was my final answer. "Look, right now, *he* . . . Charles Revson . . . doesn't take me seriously. He thinks I'm a cute blond lady who is no threat to him. He's always nice, gives me a big hello, even if he does send spies into the factory. The moment I put something on the market that competes seriously with him, he's going to get upset, get difficult. We're not big enough to fight him—yet. No nail enamel, please, Leonard.''

And we didn't. We kept a low profile, kept our sales and profits to ourselves. We stayed out of sight until we were strong enough to compete, to invite copy.

CREATE—DON'T COPY

''Imitation is the sincerest flattery,'' wrote one sage, but in my business, it's more annoying than flattering. The fragrance industry is one in which there is much flagrant imitation. The competition and, often, an eager entrepreneur will try to duplicate a scent. It can't be done. Occasionally, I'll see a street vendor selling a look-alike bottle of fragrance that pretends to be an Estée Lauder scent. The packaging may be similar and the lettering may be very close, but experience the scent. If you're familiar with the real thing, even if you're not a nose, you'll know a copy when you run across one. An imitation never measures up to the original. It's the difference between champagne and ginger ale—both have bubbles, but one tastes flat after you've tasted the other.

A fragrance, like a brilliant piece of music, is a complex creation. Harmonious elements ring true. When I ''compose'' a scent, I play many diverse notes against one another, drawing from my chemist's battery of pure scents. Some are sweet and low. Others pungent. Others mysterious. Still others, fresh and green.

There is no way to copy an original unless you know every single element in the original. And, with my fragrances, even if you have a chemist who is a genius, you can't copy what's in my head . . . and that's where the secret, crucial, final 5 percent rests.

The next fragrance in my head was Aliage. It was sporty! I'd picked up a green leaf in Palm Beach one day, deeply inhaled its scent with wonder, and knew I had to re-create that smell. The active woman needed a scent all her own: when she went to a gym in her tennis shoes, she didn't want to conjure up a whole symphony orchestra. I could never find a scent that would be right on the tennis court, so I had to invent it. Aliage was composed of over 300 ingredients that exploded into movement and life.

Released at just the era of the great denim takeover, Aliage was meant for jeans or a tennis dress. It was fresh and green and alive.

My scents were seized by the consumer as soon as they appeared. Women were tired of the standard perfumes of their mothers' generation, the tired, familiar names, fragrances made for a generation of women who blue-rinsed their gray hair and had croquignole waves etched into their scalps. It was time for the new woman, the one who dared to buy her own perfume. This woman bought perfumes for their fragrances and for the way they fit her life-style. She would not be misled, even twenty years later, by perfumes that bore designer names. What does a dress designer know about skin scent?

Next came Private Collection. The theory of exclusivity has always worked for Estée Lauder. Women want what is not available to multitudes.

In my private office, I keep a rare collection of oils, jasmine, orange leaves, extracts, and essences from every corner of the world. I'd been working for several years on a special scent. I loved it, and kept it for myself, partly because it was unique, so discreet. I almost didn't want to share it, partly because I felt it wasn't quite ready to be marketed. I hadn't even yet thought about a name.

"What are you wearing?" I was often asked.

"This is, well, this is from my private collection," I'd respond. "It doesn't have a name. It's . . . just . . . mine."

One day, Saks Fifth Avenue called. "We've had four requests today for your Private Collection perfume," said the fragrance buyer.

"There is no such fragrance," I said, mystified.

I gave samples to my closest friends, who told their friends, who told their friends that the new scent was from Estée Lauder's private collection.

Saks called back. "That Private Collection of yours? We must have it, Mrs. Lauder!"

Just before the scent was shipped to the stores, I sent a few bottles as a gift to my longtime friend Princess Grace of Monaco, who had always been so wonderfully charming and hospitable to me. Soon after, I attended a masked ball in Europe, to which I wore a costume designed by Irene Galitzine that included a mask that covered my eyes.

"I know it's you, Estée," said a soft and cultured voice that belonged to a beautifully gowned masked-at-the-mouth woman. "I can tell it's you because of your lovely smile!" she murmured.

"And I know it's you, Grace," I responded. "I recognize your magnificent eyes."

That wasn't altogether true. She did have beautiful eyes, Her Serene Highness, but more important for identification, I recognized the ineffable Private Collection fragrance that surrounded her. For me, that identification was far more foolproof than eyes. I could mistake a pair of royal eyes but never my own perfume.

I miss Princess Grace. She was such a gentle presence, such a wonderful mother, always there with her children at poolside, piano lessons, or parties. A mother after my own heart. A lilting Irish beauty, she had fragile sensitive skin and was always wondering what I had that was new. Her very American ebullience broke through her royal seriousness when, with childlike delight, she'd tear open the beautifully wrapped gifts of cosmetics I always brought for her when we'd meet.

A mother can have eight children and no favorites (can you favor one finger over another?), but I must admit, White Linen was a particularly cherished child. The perfume is simply one of the most gorgeous, unforgettable scents in the world. I named it White Linen because I envisioned the woman who wore it as fresh, crisp, and clean.

"Big mistake, that name," said friends. "It doesn't sound glamorous enough."

One of the first things I ever learned is to pay no attention to gratuitous advice. White Linen was the *perfect* name for this scent.

Names of scents have always carried great clout. Many of my competitors felt that putting a movie star or a designer's name or endorsement on a bottle of perfume was enough to sell a hastily contrived product. The "big name" usually had little to do with the fragrance development except to lend her name and collect her commission. How could she? Her experience was with celluloid or fabric, not skin.

I have always felt that the name had to describe the scent and the woman who would wear it—not *another* woman—a glittery personality.

If there was frenzied competition in the fragrance arena, the competition often served to whet our appetites. There is something very heady, very stimulating in beating out the competition. It can exhilarate, propel. What a feeling when you hit the counters three days before a competitor!

Oddly enough, the Eastern influence appealed to Yves St. Laurent at the very same time I had begun to put out an exotic fragrance. Cinnabar was born. I see *our* Eastern-influenced fragrance as a *color*, one with deep red Oriental vibrations. Its packaging included lush silken tassels (we're very big on tassels). Neiman-Marcus offered it first.

It amused me to see that almost immediately St. Laurent's Opium came out with a tasseled necklace upon which that Eastern perfume could be dangled. Opium retailed for $100 an ounce, and Cinnabar sold for exactly half that, outselling its competition.

We had quite a battle of wills when Lauder for Men, our first men's fragrance marketed under the Estée Lauder name, was being developed.

There were those in our perfume division who were backing a certain fragrance we'd worked on for a while. Leonard and I both knew it wasn't exactly right—it was a "me too" fragrance, a derivative scent. It would have been an assured, middle-of-the-road commercial success, but you only make millions when you do something extraordinary, something no one else had ever done before. There are what we call families of fragrances, and the scent that everyone else said was perfect, wasn't. It smelled like something else—another family from which it had been derived. You can be sure that the first Lauder for Men fragrance was going to be an original.

We worked and worked. One direction of scents was too masculine. Another was too feminine. We sent our people to Europe to come back with different formula possibilities. Everyone was pushing something else. The nose and her family were adamant. Nothing was just right.

It took two years. Finally, we had it. Not a ''me too'' fragrance. The real thing.

Smell it yourself. I can't describe it.

A new scent is about to waft its way into the world from our laboratories. It will be called Beautiful. We have managed to find a way to incorporate quite literally 2,000 fresh flowers into one perfume. It is my garden of wildflowers.

GARDEN OF WILDFLOWERS

Fragrance . . . It is a miracle. Keep your fragrance on and your frowns off. Your husband will come home and feel happy. Smell wonderful when he leaves, smell a little more wonderful when he returns. Put a dab of fragrance on your pillow at night; it will cure your insomnia. Touch the lightbulbs in your house with scent and watch your rooms turn into a garden. Put an empty perfume bottle in your lingerie drawer and a drop or so of fragrance in your rinse water and smell sweet from the first layer of clothing. Touch the moving parts of your body—the crook of the elbow, the vulnerable, soft spot behind your knees, the wrist, the palm—with exquisite scent and become delicious to everyone near.

I continue inventing and perfecting fabulous scents. In New York,

Palm Beach, Cap-Ferrat, London, Paris—wherever I am at any given time assistants fly to me and we think, sniff, experiment, and name possible fragrances. At my factories around the world, technicians work out the details of production using only pure raw materials, because synthetic materials invariably smell metallic.

Metallic is not what I want. I want divine. Smell is so basic. A baby first recognizes and attaches itself to its mother through the sense of smell. Have you ever seen a new mother passing her nose lightly over the head of her baby as she prepares to nurse it? Have you ever noticed that your sense of smell is the first to awaken in the morning? And have you ever had a fleeting sense of an intriguing woman as she rushes past and leaves nothing but her unforgettable fragrance?

There is a word for those that can't hear, and it's "deaf." There's a word for those that can't see, and it's "blind." There is no word for those who can't smell and that's because I think losing one's sense of smell is too isolating even to contemplate. I am endlessly grateful for my sense of scent, which gives me more pleasure than anyone really deserves.

CHAPTER 5

MY GARDEN GROWS

I have a confession to make. I have been shockingly excessive in a particular area of my life. When it came to my children, I always overdid it. Each woman must choose her priorities, they say. I refused to choose either business or family. I wanted both. And, with both, I invested everything . . . sometimes too much. As in the box-lunch affair.

Leonard was going away to summer camp for the first time when he was seven. I don't mind telling you, I was a nervous wreck. He seemed so small. The letter from camp required that I provide a box lunch for him to eat during the train ride to camp.

Box lunch? I certainly could provide a box lunch. Just the day before, I'd bought a new traveling suit from Bergdorf Goodman. That purple box was perfect to hold Leonard's lunch. On visiting day, Leonard told me that the fifteen or so sandwiches I had packed were quite enough for his snack and, actually, somewhat more than any other mother sent.

It's not so terrible to overdo it with your children. "Whatsoever a man soweth, that shall he also reap." I believe that. In fact, I could have made it up without ever even hearing those words. They have expressed my philosophy in business, of course, but nowhere have they rung with such meaning as in the business of family.

EXPANDED FAMILIES

I hear too many superwomen say that family seems to be superfluous today. Pity. Who knows better than I how important it is to be self-sufficient? Who is more fully convinced of the value of a woman's independence? No one.

Despite my belief in independence and self-sufficiency, a family or intimate friends add so much texture to one's life. It doesn't have to be blood family . . . the family I speak of. I know many marvelous women who had "adopted" beloved friends to be the family with whom they share joys and griefs. I hate to be close-minded about it: I suppose many manage to live relatively solitary lives with happiness, and certainly there are female superachievers today who go it alone by choice. But for me, there had to be a balance of family. Joe's massive shoulder was there for me to cry on; his smile helped me to rejoice. We took care of each other's problems. If there was someone to fire, and I couldn't bring myself to do it, Joe took over. Success simply wouldn't have been as sweet nor setbacks as easy to bear if it weren't for Joe.

I believe that parents can matter to children in ways that perhaps everyone is too busy to encourage today. It is so sad to see generations alienated from one another. Family ties are not meant to choke, but there is a reason why they are called ties. You are bound to those you love, forever and always. It doesn't matter if you argue or have serious value differences at various times in life. A family should be unbreakable. I'm not suggesting that several generations live together, although that may be an option for some. Generations of families, real or adopted, should love together.

My sons are a solid link to generations past and future for me. Joe said over and over, "Whatever we put in these boys, Estée, we'll take out." He was so right.

FOLLOWING FOOTSTEPS

As a parent, you never really know that you're doing the right thing. One thing that can never be wrong is this: give your child space and reason to learn. Then, trust his judgment.

As the business grew, we cared very much about involving our sons. When we were starting out, Ronald was a small child, but Leonard worked at the office after school every day, from the time of our first sale to Saks Fifth Avenue in 1946. He delivered packages. He was our first billing clerk, typing every invoice all during the time he was in high school. He worked every summer, every free moment. One might say that as soon as he was old enough to know what a lipstick was, he was making them.

I remember, one winter, when Leonard was sixteen, we decided to go away for an extended vacation and allow him to be the plant manager. It was a risk, yes, but one has to risk to succeed. And it wasn't such a great risk. Though he was young, I knew my son's capability. We had our bags packed and were ready to go, but the "plant manager" came down with chicken pox. We had to unpack our bags and stay.

Then, Leonard began his serious schooling. After graduating from the Wharton School of Finance and Commerce at the University of Pennsylvania, he attended the Columbia Graduate School of Business. There wasn't a move he made from his early adulthood that wasn't, in some way, geared to sharpen his business skills. Joe had been sending him copies of all the correspondence at Estée Lauder that was of any import. We were afraid, I think, that Leonard would lose interest in our business as he learned there were other things to do besides building an empire. Notes from distributors, deals lost or made, letters from customers, positive and negative—all were forwarded to him at school.

We needn't have worried. Leonard always had business on his mind. Toward the end of the Korean War, he had a choice: serve two years in the Army as a clerk typist or serve three and a half in the Navy as a supply officer. For him, there was no choice. As a naval supply officer of the USS *Leyte* he handled more money and supplies in one month than our business, at the time, handled in a year. My son was preparing himself in a myriad different ways, consciously and unconsciously, to be the chief executive officer of Estée Lauder even though none of us really dreamed, at the time, that our company would have such a glorious place in the sun. Leonard's application of the professional business skills he developed in the early years brought us into the forefront of the industry.

He was so much a part of the growth of Estée Lauder that I suspect he always knew deep inside that he would go into the business. Still, I guess he had to test his wings by making a few dramatic announcements that scared his parents half to death. When he graduated from college, he announced he might want to work in a retail business. My heart sank. Joseph was calmer.

"It's up to you, of course," Joe said to his son. "But why waste all your good knowledge and talent on a department store instead of placing it in a business that will someday be your own. The important thing, though, is for you to be happy. You must make up your own mind."

"Incidentally," I informed Leonard, "I've received an offer from Sam Rubin of Fabergé to buy us out for a million dollars. What do you think we should do?"

Leonard thought for a minute. "A million doesn't sound like so much to me," he said.

My son has always thought big.

"I'm going away for a week, to think," said Leonard. "I'll let you know what I'm going to do when I get back."

We waited. The phrase "baited breath" took on new meaning. I was for more aggressive convincing. Joe held me back.

After a week, Leonard entered my office at nine in the morning. "I've decided. I'll work for us," he said.

Then, it was my turn to be brilliant. At 10 A.M., Joe and I were heading for Florida for a two-month vacation. I knew Leonard had to learn the ropes by himself. I knew he had to be out of the shadow of Estée.

All that waited for him was a desk with some mail on it—no one to say, "Do this!" "Don't do that!"

We had total confidence and always expected that Leonard would know precisely what to do. As it turns out, our confidence was not misplaced. He was a natural at the business.

He knew our products and from the years of studying our correspondence, he understood the essence of the business. From his schooling and from the professional management skills he learned in the Navy, he had prepared himself to take risks and to make decisions. "Chance favors the prepared mind"—it bears repeating. In 1957 our company had just broken $800,000 in total sales. After Leonard was discharged from the Navy in 1958, he came to work full time, and we shared a tiny office.

Things have certainly changed. Between then and now, Leonard established a sales force where none existed, created our first research and development laboratory, where none had existed, brought in professional management on every level, and made Estée Lauder a company of international repute. By using print and television advertising, he built our business account by account, city by city, country by country. No business of any size or worth is ever the work of just one person; a skilled cooperative effort is always necessary for survival and growth. Leonard Lauder sets the Estée Lauder pace.

It hasn't always been smooth going as you undoubtedly read between the lines. The distance between parents and children often seems immense. There were many heated discussions, some more heated than others—but that proves my point. A family can disagree and still be loving. Individuals can have different approaches, but if the goal is the same, there are clear merging points. My garden was healthy and there was room for fresh blooms and new growth.

Our earnest wish was for both our sons to be involved in our business, but every wish can't be a reality. Ronald, who is eleven years younger than Leonard, has chosen public service and is currently working for the government. I'm immensely proud to have a son who is deputy assistant secretary of defense for European and NATO policy. In my heart of hearts, I'd still prefer him to be in the family business. It would be dishonest of me to say otherwise.

We tried. When Ronald graduated from the Wharton School of Business, we sent him to work in our Belgian factory. There, he attended the International School of Business in Brussels. He moved on to Paris and the Sorbonne, where he earned a degree in French literature. His skills and inclination led him to international management.

When Ronald was very young, he and Joe would spend hours at the museum—every museum. He'd come back from trips abroad with ancient armor or exquisite drawings. His taste is magnificent. When he joined our business, where he worked for seventeen years, he brought his fine taste with him. Since he had lived and studied and worked in Europe, he had developed a sophisticated understanding of the European market. He spread goodwill as he sold the Estée Lauder message in a diplomatic, yet businesslike manner. Having mastered several languages, he welcomed our European business contacts in their own languages. His superb judgment in fine art influenced our packaging, containers, and even the look of the counters to make our line not only visually exciting, but artistically innovative. He kept us true to the historical periods we chose for promotions. It was his eye that helped to create the taste-making look of our company.

You can see why I want him back in the business . . . even though I know what a contribution he is making to the country.

It was Ronald, more than anyone, who made Clinique into a profitable business. He organized the sales forces into cohesive groups. He traveled to every city in America to tell the Clinique story. His talent was political in the finest sense of the word "politics," that is, he was a master of prudent judgments and could convince others of the wisdom of his decisions.

TOUCH,
TOUCH,
TOUCH…

The *Harper's Bazaar* editorial endorsement that created a buying storm.

The Egg and Estée Lauder

✦ Estée Lauder's clients have long claimed that her creams were "good enough to eat" besides being immeasurably good for complexions. Her latest cream is a genuine innovation—includes in its formula the whole egg, reinforced with ingredients which act on the skin like hormones, but which are not. Its effect—a lovely dewy freshness; and in time an effective blandishment against wrinkles. A soft, unquestionably beautifying cream. The name—Estoderme. $6.50, plus tax.

Reprinted from the October, 1951, issue of **HARPER'S BAZAAR**

Our first big counter display on evening makeup.

Dallas *Morning News*

At La Scala Opera House in Milan, the night it was decorated in Estée-Lauder-blue–tinted flowers.

Receiving the French Legion of Honor was a high point in my life.

On my way to break new ground in Europe.

Kings-way Photographers

Even in the early days, my office always had
a very feminine touch. I created fragrances
with bottles labeled in code, I checked packaging possibilities, I planned campaigns. It
was a well-used office.

Driving along the highway, it is still a thrill for me to see my name on this plant.

I supervise every step of production with a hands-on approach as we stir the great vats of cream, check the lipsticks and packaging, and take care of whatever else is on the plant agenda.

Offices should reflect the tastes of the people who work there; they should be inviting semblances of home, not cold stereotypes of offices.

My office is soft and feminine.

The executive dining room is distinctly lush.

Leonard's office is masculine.

Introducing Private Collection
to the French press.

Teaching my saleswomen
to sell.

Enter our
Spring Garden of Fragrance
from Estée Lauder . . .
dozens of wonderful ways
to wear and give
Youth-Dew, Estee, Azuree and Aliage

Jean-Pierre Grisel

I've captured Cardinal Cooke's attention with
J.H.L.   Ed Koch is next!

The design for containers and papers often comes from extraordinary inspirations. This is an antique chatelaine the mistress of a castle carried as she went about her chores. Hanging from the chain are snuff bottles, tiny scissors, thimbles and various trifles she might need during the day. We used the objects as designs for solid fragrance holders; ours are placed next to the originals.

The Aramis paper was derived from the design on an old tortoiseshell fan.

These are our porcelain eggs, used to contain fragrance. They were inspired by the magnificent eggs of Fabergé. The Duchess of Windsor kept our eggs next to the real ones.

Joe loved this fragrance, which
was named for him.

Joe's stunning dressing-gown
fabric was the inspiration of
our J.H.L. fragrance wrapper.

—The "catchline" for this Cinnabar launch was 'MEN LOVE CINNABAR.' Note the tassled necklaces that reflected the Cinnabar wrapping.

—At B. Altman department store, in 1975. These young women are promoting a springtime garden of fragrance.

At the party that launched "Lauder for Men." *Left to right*: Director of Design, Ira Levy, Evelyn and me. The most handsome men in town showed up!

The advertisement that made the product a star. Penn's famous TWICE A DAY advertisement for Clinique was displayed in The Museum of Modern Art.

Photographed for Clinique by Irving Penn © 1974

Twice a day.

Twice a day.

Clinique is the skin care system women believe in because it works. Clinique's dermatologists worked it out this way. 3 products, 3 steps, 3 minutes, each morning and night. Clean with Clinique's great soap. Clear away with a clarifier for your skin type. Replenish with moisturizer. That's it. That's all. For skin that just gets better and better looking. Every day of your life. All Clinique products are allergy tested and fragrance free.

The feel and the look of a bottle sells cologne almost as powerfully as the distinctive fragrance. Packaging is an enormously important resource in any sales effort. Note that the women's fragrances are packaged in ethereally delicate but still reassuringly solid bottles. The Lauder For Men fragrance is in a bottle that's an architectural masterpiece; it feels strong in the hand. *At right,* White Linen. *Bottom left,* Lauder for Men. *Center,* Private Collection: Special Edition. *Right,* Cinnabar.

Ronald was general manager of Clinique for about four years, bringing a company that was very much in the red into the black. During this time, he began to start looking at cosmetics in a new way. Traveling monthly to Europe as chairman of Estée Lauder International, he searched to find the newest, most extraordinary products available in that part of the world. He realized there was a problem in bringing them home. Clinique was an extremely tight, well-thought-out line: to add new visions would have been excessive and gone against the very grain of the dermatologically endorsed products. Conversely, we had introduced so many new products in our Estée Lauder line that the few stellar European products Ronald had discovered would not have received their deserved attention if they'd been included under the Lauder umbrella. Something brand-new was called for. Ronald was the architect.

We'd been working for about seven years with a new electron microscope that enabled us to look at skin cells not as flat entities but as objects of color and skin health analysis. In New York, Ronald was having consultations with a French woman named Sylvie Chantecaille, an expert in the science of cosmetics, who had always been discouraged when searching for her own cosmetics. Whenever she'd search for new makeup products, salespeople would have enormous difficulty finding the perfect shades for her skin. At every makeup counter, different salespeople would prescribe different colors—none of them exactly right. With Ronald's encouragement, she developed a brilliant system of dividing colors of skin, hair, and eyes into different groups. The electron microscope enabled her to design customized cosmetics that would combine scientific analysis with new, exciting makeup products available on the market. Using scientific logic to create makeup, something that had never been done before, Ronald introduced PRESCRIP-TIVES. The products had a French flair and a scientific bent. Served by his knowledge of European and American marketing, the new line seized the imagination of customers everywhere. Furthermore, it provided us with a new location in stores—a concept that was fairly new at the time. Today, one may walk into a department store and see a Clinique counter, a Prescriptives counter, an Estée Lauder counter, an Aramis counter, a Lauder for Men counter, and various fragrance counters throughout the store. In the early years, one counter was allocated to one cosmetics company. Prescriptives obviously gave us more access to customers. Ronald brought in a group of very young, very enthusiastic and style-conscious young executives. Today, Prescriptives is the fastest-growing Estée Lauder product line. The energy and style that were present at its birth under Ronald's management are still very much in evidence today. He served our company wonderfully well as executive vice-president and as chairman of Estée Lauder International.

My world was complete with both sons following in our footsteps.

If my world was complete, Ronald's was not. He took his expertise in finance and international business to Washington, D.C., where he works and writes. My loss is the country's gain.

Ronald recently wrote a book called *Fighting Violent Crime in America*. Original and thought-provoking, it was highly acclaimed by the media. It details his blueprint for using business expertise to help law enforcement make our streets and homes safe. His theory is that the same advance technology used at Estée Lauder and other successful business corporations can be employed in the fight against crime.

WEIGH YOUR WORTH

You know what spurred him to write it? Something terrible that happened to me!

The doorbell rang at my home one day. Two men in Halloween masks burst in, tied up the butler, the maid, and a very alarmed Mark Hampton, the famed interior decorator, who had just arrived for an appointment.

"Where's the good stuff?" one robber demanded.

Contrary to popular belief, my whole life did not flash before me. But a very clear picture of my friend the Begum Aga Khan did. Her husband had been the leader of 20 million Ismaili Muslims. On his birthday every year, he was weighed against an equal-in-weight pile of gold, diamonds, and platinum, once tipping the scales at 234½ pounds of Aga and 234½ pounds of precious metals and jewels. (In his favor, let it be said that the money, raised from his followers, was used for charities.) At any rate, the Begum is fabulously wealthy. Once, when she was driving out of her gate, her car was stopped by armed men. Since she was leaving on a long trip, her jewels and furs were in the car. The robbers evidently knew the car would be filled with dazzle.

"Where's the good stuff?" the robbers asked the Begum.

"In my mind," the Begum later recounted to me. "I weighed the 'good stuff' against my own weight—and I weighed more. I gave them everything."

With a gun at my head, I weighed the "good stuff" against my own weight and I, too, weighed more. If the valuables in my home had weighed 10,000 pounds, I would have weighed more.

I gave them everything.

Then activated the secret alarm. The police arrived two minutes afterward.

Ronald thought I was more plucky than wise in ringing the alarm. But what really provoked him was the sense of helplessness we all felt at of my being victimized in my own home. It spurred him on to research and to articulate deep convictions that there was a businesslike way of squelching crime.

MOTHER-IN-LAW MESSAGES

My sons have made full and productive lives for themselves. They've married wonderful women; love flows through all our homes like fresh air. I believe in love. If you love someone, take the best from him, never the worst.

It seemed quite natural for me to slip into the role of mother-in-law.

I cannot resist, at this point, giving advice to mothers-in-law, advice to those of you with sons, anyway. I don't know what it's like to have a son-in-law, but I get along superbly with my daughters-in-law. I've faced this fact: my daughter-in-law will never exactly be my daughter. Why should she when she has her own mother? But I've found I can be the next best thing. If you open your heart and heritage to a daughter-in-law, she'll love you for it.

My friend's son was recently married and she agonized over what gift she could buy for his new wife.

"Don't *buy* her anything," I suggested when consulted. (If the truth be told, I probably would have made my suggestion even if she had not sought my advice.) "Give her something of your own, something you cherish, the very best thing you possess, if possible. Say, 'This is mine and I want you to have it now because it means so much to me, and so do you.' "

My friend was really appreciative. She gave her son's new wife a magnificent cameo ringed with diamonds that had been in the family for generations. Though she hated to part with that cameo, she didn't look at it that way. She was gaining a friend.

If you feel no one will ever be good enough for your son, keep it to yourself. First of all, you're probably wrong. Second of all, if he's yours, she's yours. Take off your earrings, your ring, your precious family heirloom, and give it to her along with your love and trust. Trust and love are wonderful, but don't forget the earrings.

Another friend of mine has basically the same theory, but she phrases it rather differently. I pass along to you her advice to mothers-in-law. "When faced with a new daughter-in-law in your family," says my friend in a cheerfully resigned manner, "there's only one thing to do. Keep your mouth closed and your pocketbook open."

Even though your daughter-in-law can't really be your daughter, she can come very close. I feel so fortunate with both of mine. I always wanted a daughter. My sons are wonderful, but I longed for someone who could really try on my creations. I always liked to experiment on my own family, and a daughter would have been my prime model. So strongly did I feel this that when Ronald was very small, I told a lawyer I was interested in adopting a daughter. Then, with the pressure of business and the inattention of the lawyer, I forgot all about it. The day before Leonard and Evelyn were married, the lawyer called. He had a beautiful baby girl for me. He wasn't inattentive, it turned out, just a little slow. Fifteen years too slow.

"Thanks, but no thanks," I told him. "I'm getting a daughter tomorrow."

Evelyn, as a matter of fact has worked in our business from the very moment she entered the family. She's been an extraordinary asset in uncountable ways. In 1959, when she first married Leonard, she began the first training schools for the behind-the-counter Estée Lauder beauty advisers. She set up ongoing programs in every city in the country, to teach the advisers how to consult, analyze, and sell. Evelyn had been a teacher and learned to sell from her own mother in the retail business. I taught her my approaches as well. She subsequently wrote the first teaching syllabus for our program: just as doctors who take refresher courses, our beauty consultants take refresher courses several times a year to catch up on our latest products and methods. Evelyn was the first public relations director of Estée Lauder, the first new products and packaging director. Today, she travels around the world, meets the press, makes television appearances, reviews all our makeup and marketing lines, and works on new fragrances and creams with me. I gained more than a daughter when Leonard married, as I told the laggardly lawyer: I got a whirlwind.

Ronald's wife, Jo Carole, who has an art background, worked with her husband, utilizing her exceptional talents and enthusiasms. She designed our Clinique "lipstick tower," the display instrument that allows a consumer to pull out a sample and test it on herself. The tower had to be utilitarian and attractive, a display as well as a functioning apparatus—no small task to accomplish. Jo Carole's first job with our company was behind the counter at Bloomingdale's, learning first hand what the Estée Lauder customer needed. She, as well as many other executives, spent time selling so they might learn the market in the most direct way. Her lipstick tower was designed as a vertical display because she soon realized that there was a limited amount of available counter space and a horizontal piece of equipment would take up too much room.

When Clinique was launched in Philadelphia's Wanamaker's department store, Jo Carole was there selling. Father's Day in New York's Bonwit Teller also saw her behind the counter, and as a competitor ruefully commented, "You sure can't beat a family business; there's always SOMEONE there who cares." He was right. Ronald was responsible for our Bamberger's department store account, which has since grown to be one of our biggest. He and Jo Carole would visit one of the stores on Saturdays, when young people and their mothers were likely to shop. Jo Carole and Ronald would constantly devise new and ingenious methods of attracting customers to Estée Lauder. Jo Carole once created an extraordinarily successful marketing device. She arranged for a special effect: a small cart was filled with dry ice, and huge billows of attention-getting "smoke" poured out. She piled scores and scores of lipsticks on top of the ice. The cart was placed in the college clothing department just before back-to-school time arrived. I can't remember a more inviting display and young women, shopping for their new skirts and sweaters, could not resist buying lipsticks to match every outfit. Jo Carole's dry-ice cart broke records!

In the late 1960s, Jo Carole became quite active in the museum work she so loved. As a member of the Junior Council, she worked diligently and creatively, and subsequently became chairman of the Associate Council of the Museum of Modern Art.

Yes, I brag about my family! One difference between me and my sons is their modesty. Neither toots his own horn. I, on the other hand, have been known to mention my accomplishments. Also everyone else's.

I remember receiving a phone call from a friend when Leonard was attending the Bronx High School of Science in New York City.

"Congratulations," she said.

"For what?" I asked.

"Well, Leonard's winning the New York State Regents Scholarship, of course. I read it in the New York *Times* two days ago."

I ran from candy store to candy store trying to find a two-day-old newspaper. It couldn't be done. When Leonard came home, I confronted him. "What's this I hear, Leonard. Did you win a scholarship to college?"

"Yes, yes," he said with a shrug. "I didn't tell you because I knew that the moment the words were out of my mouth, you'd be on the phone to the world with the news."

Well, I couldn't see what would have been so terrible about that. When Ronald won the same scholarship, I managed to find out in time to tell everyone.

I'm gratified to see that some of my traits have sunk in, almost unnoticed, except by me. I notice everything. When Leonard was a teenager, I'd send him to camp with a few dozen self-addressed postcards—addressed to me. That's the only way I could be sure of an occasional note from him. I recently saw Leonard giving out stamped, self-addressed postcards to salespeople all over the country. In this way, he stays in touch with our most valuable asset—the sales force. A suggestion, a complaint, a comment, can be immediately forwarded to the front office as it occurs to a salesperson. That helps us stay in touch with what is happening at Estée Lauder counters nationwide and even worldwide. You never know just what will stick in the mind of your child forever, do you?

Leonard, I must admit, is more careful with money than his mother. I don't worry too much about spending money. And I never, ever cut corners to give up a particle of quality. That is how I like it.

That's why Joe was such a perfect balance for me. In the interest of quality, I would have spent too fast in the beginning. Joe tempered me.

Like his father, Leonard also proceeds with caution, although he carries the banner of excellence no matter what the cost, just as I do.

One of the most gratifying moments of my life came when I convinced my son to invite his naval commander to dinner. Leonard really didn't want to do it—he never even invited a teacher home willingly—but I wanted very much to meet the man who was my son's superior in the service.

We lived in a large, private home in the center of New York City. I greeted the commander at the door, as I always greet my guests.

"Pardon me," he said, looking upward toward the several floors of our home. "I'm looking for the Lauder residence."

"This is the Lauder residence," I replied, mystified.

"No, no—I mean—what floor do the Lauders live on?" asked the commander.

I understood. "I'm Mrs. Lauder," I said and drew him in. "Welcome to our home."

We had a formal dinner, followed by coffee in the library and a smiling confession from the commander. "Mrs. Lauder," he said to me, "I have something funny to tell you. The name 'Lauder' meant nothing to me all these months. It never for a moment occurred to me that your son was that Lauder—the Lauder whose name rests on five jars in my own bathroom. In fact, I have always thought Leonard must come from a very frugal, a very modest background. He is, as you know, in charge of our payroll department. I've never met a man who watched the Navy's money as closely as he. He never wastes one dime and doesn't allow anyone else to do so!"

On the other hand, Joe once said that when I go at a hundred and fifty, my epitaph should read:

> Here lies Estée Lauder
> Who made it
> And spent it . . .

It's difficult to teach things you care about to children without lecturing. You never really know whether you're doing the right thing or not. All you can do is the best you can do. All you can do is be there as much as possible. I did try to be there, even when it was close to impossible. You can be a businesswoman and a mother at the same time, but you can't be both at once, *visibly*. Tales from home don't sit well with business associates; nothing could bore them more. If your child has a high temperature, you take him to the doctor, you worry yourself sick over it, but you smile at the meeting. You never talk temperature or play group or college with the buyer. Unless, of course, you're talking about his child's play group. Then, the rules change.

I've always found it best not to press. Joe taught me that. It hardly ever works to press your child into doing what you want him to do. I remember that Leonard was determined to go to the Wharton School of Finance and Commerce because business was always on his mind, even though he wasn't sure what business it would be. We thought it would be wonderful for him to become a chemist—that would work so well with our business. Joe would take the classified sections of the Sunday paper, when Leonard was in high school, and he'd say, "*B*, look under *B* for Businessman, Leonard. See how many people are looking for businessmen? *None!* Now, look under *C* for Chemist. Everyone wants chemists!"

Leonard went to Wharton, nevertheless.

GENERATIONAL GOODNESS

Each generation of my family brings new dimensions and new energy to what began as a little girl's insatiable love of beauty in all things.

They're all gone now—the people who founded the great companies of beauty. Only I am left. Revson was replaced by that fine gentleman Michael Bergerac. Elizabeth Arden left her company in turmoil when she died in 1966 without having set her affairs in order. When Helena

Rubinstein died in 1965, Colgate-Palmolive took the reins until 1980. Charles of the Ritz is now owned by Squibb, Germaine Monteil by Beecham, and Max Factor by Beatrice.

The personal love and involvement are gone; they're companies now, not a family's heart and soul.

It won't happen to Estée Lauder.

Our company has developed a life and momentum all its own—a dedication to the dream. There's a whole new generation waiting to take the reins of Estée Lauder when its turn comes. My two grandsons, William and Gary, and my two granddaughters, Aerin and Jane, are sharpening their skills and their passions for excellence. They have beauty on their minds.

Recently, Aerin called me on the telephone. "Estée," she said (that's what everyone calls me—why not her?), "I couldn't sleep last night because I was so excited. I've got a *wonderful* name for a new perfume! How about Dreams. Wouldn't that be just lovely? Or how about Été . . . it means summer. Oh, I LIKE Été!"

I have everyone doing it. My garden grows.

PART TWO

MAKING
THE DREAM
COME TRUE

CHAPTER 6

BREAKING NEW GROUND

Estée Lauder was becoming a household word. "Follow the Lauder" is the way the media referred to my growing success, but it was growing just in America. I was small and blond, but I began to think about applying weight to breaking new ground.

Still, it was Leonard who first said, "I want to go international."

Fresh from a stint in the Navy and a tour on foreign soil, he became convinced that the European woman was not only fashion-conscious but face- and body-conscious, even more so than the American woman. She spent much more money for makeup than her American counterpart because she was in pursuit of quality and purity and not just beauty. It was *her* mother who first discovered mud baths, mineral baths, and purse-depleting body spas. In America, the girl-next-door look was the rage. In Europe, "natural" took a back seat to being glamorous and finished in style.

We were determined to break ground in a foreign market. In our favor was the fact that European business people were interested in quality. Few talked money—only purity. They reflected the taste of their customers. We were expensive but decidedly pure.

I bided my time and waited for our reputation to knock at doors across the sea. It didn't take too long.

BEAUTY AND THE BEST

I was convinced that my marketing strategy in America would also work abroad. If I could start with the finest store in London, which was Harrods, all the other great stores would follow. Fashion cachet would only come through the best outlets. It would be much harder to aim for the stars in Europe than to break through in second-rate department stores. Still, if I placed my products in a lesser atmosphere, they would be tainted with second-class citizenship.

As luck would have it, Sir Richard Burbridge, the owner and director of Harrods, came to visit his good friend Mr. Adam Gimbel in New York.

Sir Richard asked Mr. Gimbel if there were any exciting new products on the market. Mr. Gimbel told Sir Richard that there was a new cosmetics line in the store that was selling brilliantly. He went on to say that it was owned by a woman who could sell a defunct railroad line in about five minutes. Sir Richard decided to see me. It was 1959. I was in my tiny office at 15 East Fifty-third Street when I received a telephone call that a Sir Richard Burbridge of Harrods in London, England, would like to meet me.

I could hardly contain my excitement.

Sir Richard did come. He told me that Adam Gimbel never raved about anything. Since he was raving about Estée Lauder, Sir Richard would like me to stop in to see his buyer the next time I was in London.

I put some cream on Sir Richard's hand. I gave him some to take home to his wife. Yes, indeed, I assured him, the next time I was in London, I'd contact his buyer.

I found myself in London almost immediately.

"Sir Richard suggested I see you," I told the Harrods buyer. "He thought my products would be just right for Harrods."

Not so simple. Nothing is ever simple. What a blunder. I'd gone over her head and bypassed channels by speaking to the buyer's boss before I spoke with her. She wouldn't give me the opportunity to say two more words.

Simply not interested was the unmistakable message.

Selfridge's was available to me, but it wasn't the most prestigious store in London at that time. I turned them down.

A little media attention was called for. I visited the beauty editors of various magazines. I was especially interested in the British edition of *Harper's Bazaar*, a guidepost to excellence. The editor at *Harper's Bazaar* was very kind and said that she knew and admired my Super-Rich All Purpose Creme. Carmel Snow always brought her a jar whenever she came to London. Yes, she'd be happy to write a piece about my products; what store in London would be carrying them?

"My products are not available in London," had to be my reply.

"Well," she answered, "I'll write a piece saying that Estée Lauder's cosmetics will be coming soon."

"Wonderful," I said, and gave her a jar.

Beatrice Miller was the beauty editor for *Queen* magazine. "May I just put a bit of cream on your skin to show you how fresh and lovely it will make you feel?" I asked her.

"You certainly may not," said Beatrice Miller.

But in walked her secretary with very troubled skin. She was willing, thank goodness. Before she could say much more than a rather doubtful "Well, I suppose you could try," I was in action.

I had a little box of products with me, which I used on her face. You could see a difference in only five minutes. I can see that girl's face in front of me right now—her name was Penny—and even Beatrice Miller was impressed. *Queen* magazine came out with a fine article, but we still had no place in London where customers could find us.

Again I went to Harrods.

"I'm not trying to sell you something that isn't the finest," I told the buyer. "I'm trying to sell you something I think the American visitors to London will appreciate having accessible and a product that the Englishwoman needs to know about!"

Again the answer was no. There was no space at this time, there was no call for my products, this wasn't the right time of the year, maybe another time . . .

I had committed a fatal error by speaking to her boss before approaching her. I wasn't sure I could redeem the mistake, but I had to keep trying. Since this incident, I always tell salespeople never to go over the buyer's head. See the one directly responsible for the cosmetics department, not the boss. Let the buyer get credit! Another lesson learned—the hard way.

I stayed in England a month, visiting every beauty editor to make my name known. I was getting write-ups but no Harrods order. Before I left London, I visited with the buyer one more time. "Can't you just take the smallest order," I asked. "Or even let me send a supply of my products to your home so you can experiment and see for yourself how good they are."

"No, no, no, send me nothing."

Harrods was looking very bleak.

The next year, I went back to London. And Harrods.

I think the cosmetics buyer must have been reading the magazines, and my friends, the beauty editors, had been so supportive. She was not quite as hostile, not quite as intractable. "Let me tell you, I have no room here, as I've told you before," she said brusquely. "But perhaps I could take a tiny order and put it in with the general toiletries. It won't be next to the good cosmetics—that you'll have to understand, Mrs. Lauder."

"Oh, I quite understand," said I, nearly bursting with joy. "Wherever you say will be just fine."

"We don't run ads, we don't have promotions, we won't give a gift with the customer's purchase. I hope you understand that."

I did.

Estée Lauder appeared, almost invisibly, at last.

It was not a victory yet. I visited every one of the beauty editors again, to remind them of me. Another round of makeups. Another round of samples. "Do you think you might write another piece?" I asked each one. "Now that we're in London at Harrods?"

The articles appeared.

Customers also appeared. I was on my way. Women began asking for Estée Lauder. The Harrods buyer was reluctant to notice, but she had no choice.

In the flush of a good week's sales, I summoned up courage to ask if she could give me a more important counter. "This is such a good line. You see how it's moving, and we have a wonderful new fragrance called Youth Dew . . ."

As I spoke, I dared to open a bottle and quickly touch a drop—just a drop—of Youth Dew to her hand; it could make her furious. It might—just might—pique her interest. A calculated risk.

"What's this all about?" she asked with some irritation.

"Youth Dew is about a bath oil that doubles as a skin perfume; it's nondrying and it's taking America by storm. Please, won't you take this bottle home?"

"Oh, no," she said, "I never do that. You should know that by now, Mrs. Lauder. And other counter space is definitely not available."

But I left the Youth Dew on her desk. And she pretended not to notice. I will never know if she took it home. About six months later, I made my third trip to London.

"Well, we seem to have many London women asking for your products," she grudgingly admitted. "I think I'll give you a small spot at a more prestigious counter."

And that's how Estée Lauder came to Europe. Fortnum and Mason followed, and Selfridge's, along with many other branches of Harrods. Eventually, we appointed an exceedingly talented person to head the British expansion. Under Roy Harrington's leadership, Estée Lauder became the largest cosmetics company in all of England. I went from one store to another to train my salespeople. I worked day and night, night and day, to make our line a success in England.

PARLEZ-VOUS LAUDER?

France was another story. In France, they thought they knew everything and had everything they needed. Nothing that America had would interest a French woman. I tried to sell Youth Dew to Galeries Lafayette, one of the great department stores in France, and the buyer would have none of it. Youth Dew . . . when there was Chanel? The buyer wouldn't see me.

I became friendly with one of the girls who was selling something else. While I was showing her my Youth Dew, a good bit of the bath oil spilled on the floor. They said later that I did it on purpose. I'll never tell.

I just left it there. Customers came and went. The fragrance was sweet and heavy in the air.

"What is that scent?" asked many.

"I don't know," replied the salesperson. "A woman from America was showing it to me. She accidentally spilled some on the floor. That's what you're smelling."

Whenever the buyer passed the counter, all that day and the next day as well, that beautiful fragrance lingered. He also overheard all the customers asking, "What's that I smell?? It's gorgeous!!" (in French naturally).

Finally, the French understood I was selling something other than treatment products. Actually, I think they owe me a great debt. Perhaps it sounds immodest, but I have no doubt that I expanded the perfume market significantly by convincing women they didn't have to wear perfume only on special occasions but could wear it every day of their lives. This helped the elegant French perfumers, as well as me.

Whenever I have a fragrance promotion today, I ask my salespeople to spray some scent on the counters and in the air to attract the customer. I notice that many large department stores have set up a system that wafts fragrance into the air through specially designed ducts during a promotional period. My little Parisian "accident" set the stage.

We opened in France soon afterward.

Raymond Bermay was the brilliant director of the French launch, and nothing about that was easy. Imagine trying to sell American products to the French, who'd held the banner of excellence and prestige for years.

THE TERRITORY GROWS

I remember the thrill of opening our Belgian factory. I literally broke the ground with a shovel. The Belgium representative gave a stirring speech to hundreds of schoolchildren who'd gathered, saying, "This lady is bringing a beautiful scent to our land." (I brought quite a few beautiful cents, as well, I might add.) "When you grow up, you won't have to leave our land for America to find work. There's a nice place to work right here for you."

It was a nice place to work. For blocks around the factory, the air smells sweet. I loved the children of Belgium and I'm thrilled to have played a small part in the commercial development of their country.

In the sixties, Austria was a blank patch on the cosmetics map. Most women made do with soap and water and one all-purpose face cream. As for men, Old Spice was the only brand to offer a complete range of products. Today, our products are sold in every exclusive perfumerie in the capital. And Austrian men smell better, Austrian women look prettier. Ronald's lifelong friend Dr. Peter Kurtz was appointed to build Estée Lauder in Austria, and he's succeeded brilliantly!

Canada. Canada was not easy. I went to Simpson's in Toronto, the grand store, where the buyer told me he had no more room for new cosmetics and, anyway, their entire cosmetics budget was already allocated to their old customers.

I didn't answer, just took out a bottle of Youth Dew and put a drop on his hand.

"Smells nice, but sorry," he said.

"You need a bath oil," I told him. "Women would love to come into a department store instead of a drugstore to buy it. Look, buy it on consignment. If you sell it, fine. If you don't, you've lost nothing."

"Oh, okay," he said. "But send me just a few bottles. And only the oil."

So, as I was wrapping the bath oil to send from New York to Canada, I decided to put in a few creams with a note: "Take these on consignment also. You certainly wouldn't want to have to say no to any woman who asks if you have anything else in this line, right?"

"What about our exclusive with the other company, what about my lack of space, what about . . . what about . . . ?" he sputtered when I spoke with him later.

"Look, you must go with the trend, with the world," I said. "Everyone is using this bath oil and these creams in America. You don't have to pay me for them until you sell them.

"Oh, okay," he said in resignation.

When I came to make a personal appearance at the opening of Estée Lauder in Canada, my sales department had sent everything. The bath oil, the cologne, the Estoderme Youth-Dew Cream, the Emulsion. And little boxes of powder I could give away as gifts.

We sold out everything.

"The buyer came down to see me after three or four days. "How did you do it?" he asked.

"Never mind, I did it. And I'm sending you more."

"You don't sell cosmetics," he responded. "You sell yourself."

We opened in Canada.

When we opened in Italy, the Italian women were gorgeous, and seductive. They were sophisticated with the use of makeup—their main emphasis was eyes (think of Sophia Loren), but they were not very aware of skin care. I brought them Creme Packs. The smoldering eyes of the Italian woman stayed smoldering and her skin cleared up noticeably. Leonard hired an extraordinary gentleman named Hans Thalman to expand our Italian base, and business soared.

About this time, Robert Worsfold, a multitalented organizer, was chosen to foster Estée Lauder development. Bob eventually became the founder of Estée Lauder International.

The Orient, Japan specifically, was converted to our line through the efforts of a wonderful German gentleman, Fred Langhammer, who, of course, speaks fluent Japanese.

Today, we do half of our total sales volume abroad in seventy-five countries, at last count—all of Europe, Japan, Singapore, Hong Kong, Australia, Venezuela, Canada, Mexico, wherever they care about looking lovely.

Together, my family and I shepherd this splendid company to exotic as well as familiar places. Together we spread the word that pure is best, and Estée Lauder products are synonymous with purity.

CHAPTER 7

REAL MEN USE SCENT

In 1964 you can be sure a man was a man. He thought that meant being a tough guy. And being a tough guy meant that he would never buy anything advertised as a toiletry or cosmetic.

"Toiletries? For women!" scoffed one interviewer to me on a television show shortly after we launched Aramis for men.

"Do you use a shaving cream, sir?" I responded quickly. "A shampoo? A soap? An after-shave lotion? And tell me honestly, after a day's sail, when your hands are rough and reddened, haven't you ever crept into your wife's side of the medicine cabinet and borrowed her hand lotion? They're toiletries, pure and simple!"

Nevertheless, the marketplace was barren in the men's toiletries field. The products available for men were mediocre at best and irritating at worst. I liked men, in fact, loved them, particularly my own three—Joe, Ronald, and Leonard. I was beginning to feel they were underprivileged. In the winter, Joe would come in from a brisk walk with a red and raw face.

"Please use some of my face cream," I begged. "Here, I'm turning into a cosmetics tycoon and my own husband's face *hurts*."

He declined all offers. I knew I'd have a difficult time selling skin care to men if my husband's behavior was any indication of masculine reluctance. Well, here was another challenge I couldn't resist.

I was also not satisfied with the way most men smelled. Joe's after-shave lotion was mostly alcohol—nonsoothing, nonpleasing, definitely not terrific. The lotions used in barber shops were either sickeningly sweet or smelled strongly of chemicals. Hair lotion for the rich and famous as well as the poor and not so famous was Vitalis. If ever there was a real need . . .

"Stick to what you know. Women's cosmetics!" More gratuitous advice from well-meaning friends and advisers. Well, what I knew was skin. And skin was genderless.

I called my forces into play and focused on Leonard and eight other men in the firm. For eighteen months each of them took over the shelves in their bathrooms—shelves previously occupied by their wives' toiletries.

The nine men tried out every conceivable formula needed for shaving, after shaving, and masculine skin care. They were guinea pigs for me, shampooing sometimes up to six and seven times each evening in bathrooms that now looked like laboratories.

In 1965 we launched Aramis. Its packaging—a brown paper with an Estée Lauder blue stripe—was fairly uninspired. Aramis consisted of three products: a fragrance, a cologne, and an after-shave lotion. Leonard and I were somewhat hesitant about including the after-shave. We worried that this weaker version of the fragrance wouldn't project enough to compel men to return for more. I always say a fragrance has to "lift" off the skin; it can't just sit there dully. The line, sorry to say, didn't sell.

In 1967 we decided to relaunch the product. We had never had a flop. We believed we had a great concept in Aramis and we couldn't let it die.

Instead of simply relaunching the product in different packaging, we decided to pioneer a new idea in men's treatment—a master plan for skin. An entire line of men's products had never been born intact before. In addition to the after-shave and cologne, we included a pick-up masque, eye pads, after-shave moisturizers, and a special shaving formula. The master plan was unique. It was a series of lessons for men on how to best care for their skin.

We also changed the look of the line. The Aramis products, you'll note, are packaged in tortoiseshell wrappings. I had a magnificent tortoiseshell fan. The design always seemed so richly masculine to me. Everyone said, "Too busy, Mrs. Lauder. It will detract from the bottle to have all those shadings of brown and gold on the package." I wasn't interested in a committee vote. When I knew something was right, I ran with it.

At an international sales meeting in Cannes, we came up with the final bottle design. During one of the coffeebreaks, Joe, Leonard, Elaine Marstad, head of the package development department, and I looked at the new bottle. We didn't like it. It was too square and thus wouldn't have a broad facing on the countertop. We stuck with the old, rectangular-shaped Aramis bottle, but discarded the old cap and chose a newer, sleeker one. We okayed the tortoiseshell paper for the last time— and we were in business.

We wanted to launch Aramis with the prestige it deserved—in *The New Yorker* magazine. *The New Yorker* had to be convinced that the new products were neither dangerous nor experimental before they'd accept the advertisements, and a committee came to our offices to hear Leonard's presentation. The screening process was stringent, but Aramis passed muster.

The headline of the first ad that ran in *The New Yorker* was, THE HANDS THAT CAME IN FROM THE COLD. Of course, we were selling our All-Weather Hand Cream. Ads for other products followed, and Aramis became an instant success. Originally, the line was launched with the Estée Lauder name on the back of the package. As time went on, the products developed a life of their own and now Aramis is just Aramis.

The name "Aramis," incidentally, has an interesting background.

Most people assume we got it from the dashing character named Aramis in Dumas' *Three Musketeers*, but Aramis is the name of an exotic Turkish root originally used for its aphrodisiac qualities. Well, why not? I remember one top executive saying to me, "Scent is the way to attract girls—like having money or tickets to the theater."

Our scientists were instructed to come up with more men's preparations that would soothe and protect, just as women's products did. Man's eternal struggle with his beard needed a little help with night creams, beard softeners, refreshants. Once we were in motion, we left no stone unturned. Shaving preparations included styptic creams and blemish disguisers. There were hair-grooming products and bronzers (men ought to look like winners and there's something very winning about a healthy-looking bronze tan). Shampoos, deodorants, colognes, sports' creams, followed. The potent-peppery Aramis scent came to symbolize masculine success.

It was a gamble. The American male, content with his mediocre colognes and shaving creams before 1965, was in an "I'd rather fight than switch" mode. Promotions, advertising, masculine-looking models, worked to eliminate the negative connotation that men's toiletries previously carried. All I had to do was to get a man to try Aramis—he'd change his mind about men's toiletries.

Razor rash was a thing of the past. We moved slowly, as usual. Since we were a family-owned business, since we didn't have investors to contend with, we didn't have to apologize to anyone if we didn't show immediate profits. New lines and new forays like Aramis cost money in research, design, and promotion. It could take four or five years to turn a new venture from the red into the black. Getting Aramis on the counter cost about $250,000, not an insubstantial amount of money in those days. Of that amount, $20,000 was spent on package design. This is not a completely utilitarian society. There's a certain total pleasure in the look of a product. It is a sales tool.

We didn't make that $250,000 back in the first year, I can assure you. I believe only a privately owned company could consider risking a large amount of money on a new, untried product like a men's toiletries line. If shareholders were involved, we'd have to show a steady, inexorably upward rise in profit if offering prices were not to be affected. Joe always told me to move slowly. We could afford that luxury because we owned ourselves, and always will, as long as I have something to say about it.

I admit it was difficult to get men interested in personal freshness, fragrance, and skin care products, but the market is growing as men have come to understand that smelling good and having skin that's comfortable and pliable is not effeminate but smart. Dermatologists have jumped on the bandwagon, noting that men need sunscreen products just as much as women do. Of course, if the skin is dry and sensitive, fragrances and detergent soaps are to be avoided. Instead, fragrance-free products and moisturizing soaps are required.

We have recently launched Lauder for Men, the men's line that bears the Lauder name—that's how sure of its success we are. It consists of a clean, fresh fragrance that gives a champagne lift to skin, as well as of serious treatment products. What a bottle it comes in! We used designers on three continents to come up with delightfully sturdy yet architecturally graceful lines that will be not the least of its selling tools. I've taught my salespeople to dab a bit of Lauder for Men fragrance on the palms of women who come to look.

You can't sell if you can't smell, I've told the sales force. If I come into Bloomingdale's, I expect to see my people being lavish in their efforts to get everyone to experience the fragrance rather than judge it abstractly.

Did you know that most men's colognes are bought by their women? That's because their women know what's best for them. I remember, not so long ago, experimenting with a new men's fragrance and asking Joe to try it out for me. At the April in Paris Ball, he seemed to be spending an inordinate amount of time on the dance floor. I wasn't terribly happy.

"Where have you been so long," I asked when he finally returned.

"It's your fault," he answered. "Every woman I dance with says she can't leave me because I smell so intoxicating. Imagine that! I even had to promise I'd get you to send some to my last partner's lover. Imagine that!"

I knew I had a good thing. I named the fragrance J·H·L, after Joe, who was inspiring so much excitement that night.

CHAPTER 8

BLUEPRINT OF A BIRTH: CLINIQUE

There is nothing new under the sun. Have you heard that one? Well, it's wrong. Clinique was new. Its birth was a fascinating odyssey.

Here is a truth I wish I could deny: some cosmetics provoke allergic reactions in very sensitive users. In the late sixties, there were countless women who yearned for cosmetics that their sensitive skins could tolerate, cosmetics that had fashion cachet as well as gentleness. In the industry there had been a few unsuccessful attempts to deal with the problem by producing cosmetic and treatment products from which known sensitizing agents were eliminated. The results looked and smelled medicinal. Women with sensitive skin didn't want to be left out when the newest fashions in faces came to town, but what they got were horrid colors and runny textures that reeked of therapeutics.

Leonard said it many times: if ever there was a brand-new concept that could compete with Estée Lauder, he wanted Estée Lauder to introduce it. It was evident to him that there was a large vacuum in the market that needed to be filled. Someone had to develop a line of beautiful products for those who had problems with even the finest cosmetics. Here was a place for a clever company to jump in and satisfy the need. Why not, he reasoned, jump in first—and be the *best*? Startlingly new and effective ideas were called for. No stopgap measures would do.

We were familiar with the mundane products already available. The few companies that ventured forth with lines they claimed were "non-allergenic" offered dreary, Doc-the-Pharmacist choices. There was no fashion, no glamour, no jewel-like colors—only poor substitutes that were sold mostly in drugstores and were frustratingly unsatisfying to women who cared. A word was coined about this time to describe the new cosmetics effort: "hypoallergenic," which meant that the product was likely to have an irritating effect on very few people. No responsible company ever promises its products will be totally nonallergenic, one never knows what infinitesimal particle may irritate someone's skin—somone out of millions. In the early days, though, the Doc-the-Pharmacist companies promised the moon and delivered goods that were distinctly less celestial.

Revson decided not to enter the competition at all and solemnly pronounced that "hypoallergenics is a drag."

We did not agree. What a service we could provide if a very real need in the cosmetics market could be filled by a dramatically different line of products that would be fashion-conscious and hypoallergenic at the same time.

Leonard was our catalyst. He thought this could be the biggest thing since Youth Dew. He was determined to create something strikingly original. And he, more than any of us, was convinced that if we managed to do what seemed impossible—so far, anyway—we'd not only have the first medically researched and tested fashion hypoallergenic line, we'd also have the profit of a lifetime. Without Leonard, there would not have been Clinique. At a time when I must confess I had my doubts, he insisted, he knew, we were on to something exciting and big.

In 1967 the world was changing. Women were no longer satisfied with just a touch of lipstick and a dab of perfume. So much more was available. They were beginning to understand that if they were unhappy with their features or their complexions, they could do something about it—and this did not mean surgery. There was a new sophistication about cleansing and makeup. A real consciousness raising took place when women discovered they needn't live with physical faults of body and face. The artful use of cosmetics was the answer.

But there was a group of women sensitive to almost every cosmetic. I'd always worried about them.

About this time, we had begun to hear about Dr. Norman Orentreich, a clinical and research physician of great imagination, distinction, and empathy for both male and female patients. He ran what is still one of the world's most popular skin clinics. Word had spread that Dr. Orentreich had viable treatments to retard the appearance of aging. We decided to ask Dr. Orentreich to work with our own chemists to develop our line for women with sensitive skins.

Quite apart from our efforts, *Vogue* magazine had published a series of interviews with the most important doctors of the era. In those days, doctors quoted in fashion magazines were never identified because personal publicity was considered a form of advertising and an unethical practice.

Carol Phillips, whom I'd known through my long association with beauty magazines, was the managing editor of *Vogue*. She had been responsible for the *Vogue* medical articles. The doctor she'd chosen to write the article on skin—"Great Skin: Can It Be Created?"—was none other than Dr. Orentreich. She had already begun to develop enormous respect for his ideas.

Just as the *Vogue* article on skin appeared, the Lauder family was searching for someone to head the new division we were considering. We knew we needed someone skilled in the media, skilled in beauty concepts, and willing to invest all his or her time and effort to launch a new concept. I'd always thought very highly of Carol. Since a thriving, relatively new cosmetics company was quite dependent on a friendly press, we were very cordial to magazine editors. Carol Phillips was outstanding in an exceptionally gifted group. She was bright, innovative, knowledgeable, and the perfect choice to head our new line. The question was, how could we entice her away from *Vogue*, where she enjoyed her work as well as the status of her position?

We decided it was worth a try. We approached her to say we were developing a hypoallergenic line that would be chic and would contain no known allergens. It would be, we emphasized, medically tested.

"Tested by whom?" asked Carol quite frankly. "Someone's uncle? A bought opinion?"

"No," I answered. "By Dr. Norman Orentreich's medical research facility. It already tests for the U.S. government. We've investigated this, Carol, and he's the best we can find."

We had said the magic words! We were unaware that Dr. Orentreich was the anonymous expert of *Vogue*'s popular article. The rest is history. Carol was captivated by the chance to create something truly original rather than just write about it. She joined our team as the director of the new line. With Dr. Orentreich's medically sound techniques and his research facility at our disposal, with our great understanding of makeup and skin treatment possibilities, Clinique was about to be born. Leonard's baby was to be the healthiest birth in cosmetics lore.

THE NAME

The first task was to find a name for the new line—special and quite splendid. We played with possibilities ranging from the ridiculous to the sublime.

And then, Leonard and Evelyn took a trip to Paris. They were filled with talk about the prospects of the new line. As they drove through the city, Evelyn kept noticing signs that said "Clinique Aesthetique."

Making sure every batch
is perfect.

Victor Skrebneski

Adding the secret
five-percent ingredient to a
new fragrance.

One of the most charming
first ladies who ever graced
the White House, wearing
her favorite color, with her
loving husband.

To Estée with affection Wallis Duchess of Windsor

To Esteé and Joe with warm regards

Edward Duke of Windsor 1968 Wallis - Duchess of Windsor

The Duchess of Windsor, with her beloved pugs.

This photograph of the Duke and Duchess and Joe and me was inscribed on the desk on which the Duke signed his abdication papers.

Prince Charles is a superb horseman. His wife, the lovely Diana, Princess of Wales, is his most loyal fan.

Leonard and his sons: William (*left*) and Gary.
Three men about town.

My daughter-in-law Evelyn with me.

Generational goodness.
My grandaughters Jane and Aerin.

Jo-Carole with her father-in-law Joe.

Fred J. Maroon

Tony Palmieri

A gala affair with the Lauders,
left to *right:* Leonard, Evelyn, Estée, Joe,
Jo-Carole, Ronald.

Always greet your guests at the door;
it is a warmer welcome.

Joe and I in the drawing room
of our Manhattan home.

Tony Palmieri

Tony Palmieri

Last-minute check of the tables before our Christmas party, and a close-up of a place setting; note the menu, place card and gift.

Tony Palmieri

From *left* to *right:* A friend of the Rainiers, Princess Grace, and Princess Caroline with Joe and me.

Fred J. Maroon

Everything is ready. Bring on the party!

A place setting on a highly polished
mahogany table. I adored the blue
button on the place card, making it
unique and beautiful. Use your
imagination!

Fred J. Maroon

Fred J. Maroon

Checking the drawing room before my guests arrive. Everything must be sparkle-perfect.

Cocktail hour. Light hors d'oeuvres and drinks.

Fred J. Maroon

Fred J. Maroon

Fred J. Maroon

Dinner is about to be served.

The ladies retire to the
drawing room, the
gentlemen are in the library.
This may be old-fashioned,
but it is a tradition.

Norman Parkinson

This is one of my very favorite photographs. It was taken shortly before
Joe's death, and it says everything about our great love.

She knew this meant a kind of beauty salon where women went to get facials or body treatments. It was not a hair-styling establishment, but one devoted exclusively to every type of skin care. The word "Clinique" looked wonderful to Evelyn. It was a *clean*-looking word, suggesting freshness and a clinical approach—all good. The French sound would give our products panache! When written down on paper, the C was strong and lovely. Leonard and Evelyn saw it as a motif right from the start. Clinique it would be. The name represented our dermatologically tested products perfectly and would lend glamour to them.

THE DRESS

We had another challenge. How could we make our sale experts look so different that they would be instantly recognized as Clinique people? We thought we'd look for a uniform so they would stand out as *authorities*.

A lab coat! thought Evelyn in a moment of inspiration.

It *was* inspiration, because we wanted to imply clean, laboratory conditions. And, if we added green stitching and silver buttons to that lab coat, it would look chic as well. Clinically tested and chic. That was what Clinique would be and that was the message we wanted to impart by one look at our beauty experts. A penlight that the experts would keep in their lab-coat pockets to examine carefully the customer's skin was another inspiration from Evelyn. Today, every Clinique consultant carries a silver penlight so she can evaluate *accurately* her customer's skin. It *works*, and it *looks* official, clinical, and effective.

THE MESSAGE

Why did we market Clinique under its own name rather than under the umbrella of Estée Lauder? Many people have asked me this question.

For one thing, we didn't want to confuse the customer. We were offering something new; we didn't want her to think it was like any other cosmetic she'd ever tried before. Second, we didn't want anyone to say that Estée Lauder had a nonallergenic line. It would have hurt Estée Lauder to have anyone make the very wrong assumption that we'd come out with a hypoallergenic line because there was something allergenic about our main line. Third, combining two different lines under one umbrella wouldn't allow for each to grow strongly as a separate entity. Leonard was quite correct when he said we would be our own best competition. The best way of competing was with two companies, not two products under a parent name.

100 PERCENT FRAGRANCE-FREE

My stubborness drove everyone a little mad in the beginning. I was intractable on the subject of fragrances. Or rather, no fragrances.

I knew that many allergic skin problems were caused by the perfumes most cosmetics contained. The leaders of the cosmetics companies were certain that the American woman would never accept a product that didn't smell sweet and familiar. Our product department was pushing for *natural* fragrances, like chamomile. I knew if we were going to launch Clinique, we had to do it right: 100 percent fragrance-free, 100 percent allergy-tested—*100 percent*. It eventually became the phrase by which Clinique is best known.

Clinique started with one and a half employees—Carol Phillips and half a secretary.

January 1, 1968, was the day that Carol left *Vogue* to join us. We decided that Clinique would spring full-blown in a whole line of products, not just one product, in eight months. Everyone said it was impossible—that is, everyone who didn't realize by then that we were accustomed to asking for the impossible. Carol didn't say impossible, as I remember, because as a magazine editor she was used to meeting deadlines—even killing ones.

We and our chemists had many meetings with Dr. Orentreich to plan out a line that would be hypoallergenic and still beautiful. He was such an important resource that we employed what we needed for the actual product development and had excess information to use as the basis for the Clinique informational series—educationally informative pamphlets for our customers.

TOP SECURITY TIME

The undercover operation began. If there were ever spies in the marketplace, they were everywhere now. Paranoid as that might sound, it was true. Our cover name was Miss Lauder.

Anytime anyone in the company wanted to discuss or write a memo on the gestating Clinique line, we were to call it Miss Lauder. We hoped that would imply to those who broke through our secret barriers that we were turning out a "junior" line of cosmetics. And it worked. Word drifted back that one known infiltrator was particularly puzzled at our choice of Carol, no teenager, to head the line. "What's a nice, mature *Vogue* editor doing as the spokesperson of a junior line?" he mumbled to everyone who would listen.

Actually, the security was tremendous. Clinique people worked out of 666 Fifth Avenue in a dark, cramped, tiny office on the second floor so the rest of us could dash back and forth between there and our own second-floor office without having to wait for elevators. Time was always of the essence—we were racing against a deadline. Now that we knew how explosive our project was, no one was going to come in first. A Mosler-safe lock was installed on the Clinique door. If Carol had to decide on a certain color for our package, she had to leave the windowless room, walk down the stairs, cross the street to the St. Regis Hotel, go into the St. Regis ladies' room, where, after locking the door, she could see the colors under consideration in daylight. The St. Regis ladies' room did have a window.

Each product had its own code name, which the shared secretary typed and laboriously glued onto jars and bottles. The code names were then transcribed onto sheets of secret memoranda with the real names that would eventually grace the Clinique products. These memoranda were kept locked inside a safe, to which only two or three people had the combination. Only torture could have gotten those numbers out of us.

Almost every meeting was held in the hallway because there was no time for meetings. Carol would wait for Evelyn on her way to my office. "We have to make a decision on the name for the moisturizer," she'd whisper urgently. "Have we decided on Dramatically Different Moisturizer?"

"It's a mouthful, isn't it," Evelyn would whisper back. "Maybe customers won't remember it, but, yes, it's good. Let's go with it!"

"Yes, yes, it's perfect, I'd agree" I'd answer. "Let's go with Dramatically Different Moisturizer."

Carol would waylay me in the hall. "Mrs. Lauder, we need a name for the new soap, right away! The package people are putting pressure on us," she'd say. "How about that name we discussed, Lean Forward Soap, because if you lean forward when you're soaping your face, you're going to get more circulation, more open pores?"

"No, no. It doesn't work. No Lean Forward Soap!"

And so it went.

The product was to have integrity and clarity. For the first time, we had medically tested what we were offering. "Do what is right. It will please some people and astonish the rest," Mark Twain wrote. It came to be the motto of Clinique.

Since we were such a small company at the time, everyone had something to say—everything was everyone's idea. "Who did this?" "Who thought of that?" people are always asking. Leonard had a small plaque made that reads, ANYTHING CAN BE DONE AS LONG AS EVERYONE GETS THE CREDIT. It's true. No cosmetics company in America had ever launched a complete line, full-blown. The customary marketing device was that one successful product bank-rolled another and then another. With

Clinique, we funded a full line, all at once. What a chance to take! We launched Clinique with 117 items.

THE PACKAGE

After we developed the 117 products and named them, we had to consider their packaging. This packaging really had to be "dramatically different."

At the time, Lauder packaging consisted of shades of blue with touches of gold. The logical complementary scheme for a sister hypoallergenic line would be green and silver. We had to be careful that the packaging wouldn't look too clinical or people would get the impression that only women with delicate or troubled skins were the Clinique target audience. On the contrary, we knew Clinique would be perfect for everyone and necessary for those with fragile skins. Someone brought in a swatch of material—the tiniest fruits and flowers. *Perfect*, we decided, *mille fleurs minuscule* . . . a thousand tiny flowers would be the motif. Then someone brought in a swatch of willow-green and silver paper. *Perfect*, we thought. We loved them both. What to do? We decided to have the willow-green paper for the treatment and the floral paper for the cosmetics. Tiny flowers. But then someone said, "Let's blow that pattern up." We did. It was attractive. "Let's blow it up a little bigger, then bigger, then even bigger." We experimented. Finally, the flower pattern was so large that the flower or part of a flower appeared in a different place on every package. The lack of conformity made some people nervous, but Carol and I loved the uniqueness of the concept. A glorious solution.

THE COUNTER

Everyone in the family was involved in the look of the product. Jo Carole and Ronald determined that it should be a functional symbol of the wave of a functional future instead of merely an attractive place to buy products. It was the first time we'd gone from something pretty to something pretty AND scientific—a pattern that was to be repeated when Ronald created *Prescriptives*. Even the lamp that lit the counter was a shining, silver, utilitarian, artist's lamp that would allow the customer to see her skin in an honest light. Counters were no-nonsense and decidedly frank and useful. We were selling dermatologically based products as well as glamour.

THE BOMBSHELL

In the middle of our frantic preparations came a bombshell. A letter arrived in the mail from a lawyer. It simply stated that there presently existed a brand of cosmetics called Jacquet and Jacquet, which had a product named Astringent Clinique. There would be a definite trademark violation, stated the lawyer, if we went ahead with our Clinique, as rumor had it we were about to do.

Panic ensued. We had already run the packaging through the factory with the name "Clinique" on every box. We were almost ready to roll—it was the summer of 1968—and a brick wall suddenly loomed. Well, we'd gotten around brick walls before.

Leonard called our trademark attorney, who informed him that the other company would win if it came to a fight. Leonard made a trip to see Ed Downe from Downe Communications, a media group that had acquired the cosmetics company. He offered $5,000, an enormous sum for us at the time, for the right to use the name. Downe politely said no. He was thinking more in terms of 5 percent of the royalty earned from Clinique. The two men dickered back and forth and finally a deal was struck. If we paid $100,000, we could own the name "Clinique." It was a risk and a king's ransom, but we knew we'd have to chance it. The name "Clinique" was so much a part of our plans. We arranged to pay out that enormous sum in installments. It was the best deal we ever made in our company's history. Today, Ed Downe is still very friendly with all of us and still wishing he'd stuck to his guns about the 5 percent.

COMPUTER TALK

The Clinique Computer was a major innovation. We opted for a computer long before the word became a household word. We wanted customer participation—something that would give her information about what product would work best on her particular skin. The computer asked questions to elicit basic information that most trained skin specialists use to analyze skin types today. Before Dr. Orentreich, Clinique, and the computer, no one bothered. Salespeople chose for you. The decision, in the hands of an untrained salesperson, was often not based on the customer's real need or history. Our computer, which then was just a question and answer board, took the customer's individual differences into prime consideration.

If a customer requested something that would be wrong for her, we wouldn't sell it. That is the truth. If a woman came to the Clinique counter and said, "I want that Clarifying Lotion," the salesperson was instructed to say, "Wait, wait a moment. First we have to see if your skin can tolerate it." After listening to the customer's history, she might conclude that no, the customer's fragile skin would not do well with that particular lotion.

"I want it. I'll see the manager," the customer might answer. And she would. The manager would then call Carol Phillips directly.

"Don't sell it," Carol would advise. "You'll be sorry. The customer will be sorry and we will be sorry. That lotion is only for a very strong skin."

We were resolute in this matter. Of course, we lost a few customers, who were annoyed at not being sold what they requested. Still, not only our integrity was at stake. Selling blindly and without justification was bad business and would only hurt us in the end. The customer simply wouldn't return for more bad advice.

THE CLINIQUE WOMAN

Then, we hired the six Clinique Women, staff supervisors who went on the road to open Clinique accounts in stores everywhere. Most of them were not from the cosmetics industry. They were extremely healthy-looking (pallor couldn't be tolerated), literate, ambitious young women. One was the designer Rudi Gernreich's showroom manager, another was an airline hostess, another was a teacher. Evelyn trained these women in Clinique product usage and they, in turn, trained local sales-people all over the world. The saleswoman was our secret weapon. She would have to shine like a beacon in the store. Her nails would be immaculate, her face fresh and welcoming, her manner low-key and subtle. Contrary to what you'd expect, a customer that is led to spend too much is a remorseful customer, a disappointed consumer. I did not want the "What did I need all this for?" syndrome ever to be associated with Clinique. The selling technique was the one I had been using all my life—touch the customer and encourage her to try the product on her own face.

GETTING READY TO ROLL

A nagging worry surfaced. Had we properly planned the amount of stock we needed for these first efforts? What kind of inventory did we need? A critical skill, product forecasting is a very technical and im-portant estimate necessary in the marketing of any product. If we forecast too much, we'd be choking in inventory. If we forecast too little, we'd run out of merchandise in no time at all. We spent so much money on Clinique, money that would be lost if there was not an even flow of the product into the marketplace. Risk, risk, risk—the name of our game.

September was our deadline. Soon after the Fourth of July, the packaging began to arrive on great boards that would be cut into individual units. The design was sensational—I was so thrilled with every new arrival.

Next, we had to *sell* a preview of our new computer approach to the stores and beauty magazines that would run ads.

Everyone worked at a frenetic pace. Spirits were up, then down, then up.

Finally, the moment of truth arrived. There must have been forty computers at forty different stations stocked with basic products throughout Saks Fifth Avenue the September day we opened. Everyone was there—the whole industry was curious. It was a spectacular launch! The excitement was contagious. The products flew off the counters. I spotted as many competitors as customers buying furiously.

There wasn't much press in the beginning. We rolled our opening across the country from New York to Philadelphia, to Atlanta, to Chicago, to San Francisco, to Los Angeles.

We brought the customers in with a Gift With Purchase, in color— a lipstick, as the best seduction. Everyone understands a lipstick; everyone may not understand a computer, a new skin regimen, a new concept.

We had launched what was considered an interesting and very special part of the industry, but not a line with a very broad appeal. That was the market's appraisal. Ours was somewhat different. Our intention certainly was to deal with the woman with cosmetic allergies, but, and the *but* is crucial, we never intended to be limited to just this woman. The marketplace never understood that. I felt sure we would also appeal to the woman who was just not getting a desired result from the products she was using and to the woman who simply didn't want fragrance imposed on her. There were hundreds of thousands of women out there in each of these categories in addition to the women with fragile skins.

THE COMPETITION FIGHTS BACK

The following May the man who said, "Hypoallergenics is a drag," launched Etherea, Revson's answer to Clinique. It was never in the same league. Why? Many reasons. We all thought Etherea was an awful name, a combination of ethical and ethereal, which was quite bland. The package was too violet and flat. The "medical" aspect was quite overdone. Every Etherea product was grimly sealed. That's not what women wanted. Revson made many mistakes, but his most basic was in attacking us. He should have said, "They can do it, but we can do it better!" Instead, he criticized us strongly—and the public knew better. On May 12, Revson advertised that "Etherea stands alone . . ." It just about did. All the customers were standing at the Clinique counters.

Revlon wasn't alone in imitating our idea. Around the world, no fewer than 180 copies were counted in the space of just two years. There was hardly a company that didn't imitate—whether it was our bottles, our names, our paper—with just enough of a difference to avoid litigation. Whole new companies were founded on the principle of high-fashion hypoallergenics. They all missed, because they failed to perceive the heart of Clinique. It was not a marketing device. It was an honest service.

After the launch, it wasn't always easy to get Clinique into the stores—despite our enthusiasm. Leonard went out to "store it" on the East Coast with Bob Nielsen, then head of Estée Lauder U.S.A. On the West Coast another top man, Bob Barnes, was having daily battles trying to convince our customers that a high-priced prestige, allergy-tested, 100 percent fragrance-free cosmetic would sell. Ronald moved everywhere, oversaw everyone. The pace was frantic. Major decisions had to be made almost daily and then acted upon immediately. We decided to spin off Clinique from Estée Lauder a mere two months after we first launched. We realized we could expedite production if we also had a separate facility for manufacturing Clinique. We also knew that if we built the factory and Clinique didn't work, we would surely increase our losses. We took the chance.

The goal was to be the first on the international market with Clinique—to beat out Revlon, which had launched the imitative but very competitive Etherea on May 12. On May 17, all of Estée Lauder's international executives met at Schloss Lauden on the outskirts of Vienna to discuss how best to do this. We decided to make a mad dash into the key stores of the world the following week, without fanfare, without advance preparation or publicity. We had to act. As a family-run business, we could move fast. Clinique beat Revlon by one week!

That was good, but not good enough. Although Clinique was accepted by consumers, it wasn't a successful business for the first couple of years. Then Ronald took over the reins as general manager of Clinique. With Jack Wiswall as sales manager, Ronald and Carol made an unbeatable team and business began to respond. Ronald reorganized the company in many ways and refined the business practices we had ignored in our zeal to perfect the product and win the race to the stores.

We at Estée Lauder never discuss figures publicly, but let me break this long-standing practice by doing so right here. I can't resist. After the first year or so of Clinique's growth, outsiders estimated that one day Clinique would reach $5 million in sales. To date, our figures have reached nearly $200 million. And we're still growing.

THE PERFECT PICTURE

Clinique was and is a modern classic. We have set standards. One of the highest has been in the area of the photography we used to advertise Clinique. Having come from *Vogue*, Carol Phillips was experienced with high-fashion, very artistic, very expensive photography. In 1974 cosmetics had nothing to do with high-fashion photography.

Clinique was well launched and returning money. We needed to do something daring to call attention to our classic product in a very classic manner.

Carol dreamed of having Clinique's "court photograph" taken by one of the greatest photographers of our time—Irving Penn. Irving Penn was fascinated with the project partly because, I think, his wife is a Clinique user and partly because he is enormously sympathetic to women. In order to teach consumers how to use Clinique products, we used the theme, "You must cleanse twice a day—just as you brush your teeth twice a day." Since a toothbrush came to symbolize hygiene habits, we had a huge one made up to use as a prop when we educated demonstrators for Clinique.

"We want the toothbrush in the picture," we told them.

"Ah, then we need a glass," said Penn.

I can't tell you what shopping for the glass involved. It had to be the perfect glass for the artist. Hundreds and hundreds were bought and discarded, shined and polished, before the now-famous simple glass was chosen.

I think the Clinique advertisements have been favorably received everywhere. They are beautifully stark: a pristinely clear glass holding a huge tooth brush, a line of Clinique products, the headline—TWICE A DAY—and no model. We are still-life; we almost never have used a face in conjunction with Clinique products. Why? Clinique's tone is educational, practical, not frivolous. The product is the hero. It is not to be identified with any age group. As Dr. Orentreich has said, Clinique is for people from cradle to grave. There was no reason for us to identify Clinique with an age group, a coloring, a life-style—anyone specific.

We placed our Penn advertisement first in the New York *Times*, where it belonged. It ran in a four-color spread. I don't have to tell you how expensive the entire campaign was, but there you are, another breakthrough, another victory. Not only did the Clinique ads reach out to the consumer, but they also had repercussions: they went on display at the New York Museum of Modern Art to be recognized for the treasures they are.

The Clinique success was a lesson for us: use the skills of each member of a family-run business. Each has fresh perspectives. Each one's involvement is strong if each one is busy. I created the business; at a different level, Leonard and Evelyn and Ronald and Jo Carole alone and together built one of the most successful lines in cosmetic history.

CHAPTER 9

THE SELLING GAME

The elegant porcelain eggs, trimmed in gold, etched in enamel, rested in splendid isolation on the Duchess's side table. Once the delight of royalty throughout Europe and Asia, Fabergé eggs were a rare and exquisite creation, to be treasured and displayed with pride, as the Duchess clearly was doing.

"They're magnificent," I told her. "And I'm happy to say they look like mine."

The Duchess looked at me rather oddly. Then she broke into a broad smile and confessed. "They are yours, Estée, but mum's the word!"

No, this wasn't a case of the Duchess's larceny. The Duchess was displaying my lovely copies of Fabergé eggs in which solid perfume was marketed, at a price considerably lower than the original.

It's not enough to have the most wonderful product in the world. You must be able to sell it. When it comes to merchandising, it's all in the eye.

I'm talking about image—image and packaging. In 1946 I knew everything there was to know about what I had to do. Times were simpler, television and million-dollar print advertising were not a way of life. One woman with definite ideas, pride in her product, and a hands-on approach could lay the foundation for a strong business. As the business grew, as the competition grew more sophisticated, as the possibilities for us became infinite, I knew I needed help. Those who came to work for our organization had to be the most brilliant, creative, aggressive people around. Furthermore, they had to understand and have my unwavering faith and commitment to the products. I needed to spread the message. Creating the finest perfume in the world is an accomplishment. Making people aware of its existence, let alone getting them to try it, is sometimes harder to do than to create it in the first place. The whole process is simplified if the perfume is offered in a spectacular egg that looks as if it had been wrought in the workshop of Peter Carl Fabergé. Packaging in no way dupes the customer or enhances the integrity of the product. If the product is disappointing, the customer will keep the container, which cost a considerable sum to make, and never return for more perfume, no matter what it comes in next. If the product is excellent, the customer will buy it again and even faster if it comes in yet another wonderful package that delights her eye. Both have to be the best—the product and the package.

Since we were in business on a grand scale, my next objective was to hire packagers and spokespeople who shared my vision of what made something appealing to others.

I knew one thing. My very special brand of customers appreciated quality and wouldn't accept second best. They were willing to pay for the best even if they weren't wealthy. They would do without before they bought an inferior product. In short, my customers had good taste.

Good taste meant classic design for image and packaging. There are certain building designs, works of art and music, that through the centuries have never lost their appeal because they are the highest examples of the form. I believe the taste to appreciate the classics, what is excellent in any field, lies in the psyche of most Estée Lauder customers. The Estée Lauder woman looks like a woman who appreciates the classics.

She likes to buy her cosmetics in packages that are reminiscent of the classics. Her eye is drawn to shapes and colors that are borrowed from the best of the natural world and the best that history has given us.

SELLING THE IMAGE

I saw models everywhere who were—there is no other way to put it—sex objects. They sold the cosmetics of competitors. Their subliminal message seemed to be, "Use what I use and you too will be popular, happy, gorgeous, and very active in the bedroom." They were beautiful, yes, but they were sex kittens.

I thought such a blatantly false message showed contempt for the customer. My women were too fine and, more important, too smart to be taken in by crudeness. My women were elegant achievers. They were independent.

My customer was quite aware that she couldn't become a whole other woman simply by using a certain cosmetic or fragrance. She could, of course, enhance herself, attract the man of her dreams, make herself more desirable and beautiful, but she could not totally change her personality as the competition's advertisements seemed to promise.

No, our ads were meant to say to a woman, "Are you *this* kind of woman in your heart? Then we can help you look as you should."

Our competition used many models to speak for them. We felt that there was what we came to call the Estée Lauder woman. She was one kind of woman, always, even though she could be rich, poor, younger, or older. She was classic. That never changed. She wasn't sexy one day and businesslike another. She was classic, always.

It was time to do something different again. We decided to personify our products in the vision of one woman—the same model—all the time. She would appear, this woman, in every advertisement.

We'd be taking a gamble. The public might tire of one face. I thought not.

The Estée Lauder woman has been represented over twenty-three years, starting in 1962, by five models, who appeared for us exclusively. Phyllis Connors and Karen Harris began the campaign. In 1971 Karen Graham was chosen by Alvin Chereskin, the extraordinary president of our advertising agency, A C and R. Her face, selected from a thousand or more pretty faces, epitomized a young, sophisticated woman with charm and éclat, as well as beauty. She was sensual rather than sexy. She was strong and smart. She seemed in charge of her life, which was perceived as the good life by millions of women who identified with her and strove to be like her. She could be a career woman or a homemaker, but whichever she chose, she was successful. She could be single or married, live in the city or suburbs equally well, and she had that certain, indefinable air known as class. You could tell all this from the ad in which she appeared. The ads were the brainchild of June Leaman, senior vice-president of Creative Marketing, an absolute master of advertising, who has been the maker and keeper of the image since 1962. June decided the model's real name would be unimportant because she was that Estée Lauder woman, not Lauren or Mary Lou. We didn't want the public to confuse the model with the product. It was a beautiful woman. Karen Graham fit our bill.

When Karen first appeared in our advertisements, most cosmetics companies and beauty magazine editors were choosing models who flaunted their "daring," their uniqueness. It wasn't enough just to be pretty and clean. June Leaman thought it *was* enough, and so did I. I didn't need a tiger woman to sell lipsticks.

The next time you see an Estée Lauder advertisement, zero in on it. Notice how the model is never dehumanized: we never focus in on a mouth or on eyes to the exclusion of the whole face. We see the Estée Lauder woman as a whole woman.

Our ads chronicle standards of beauty, trends in fashion, movements in interior design, and changes in life-style. Twenty-three years ago, the woman in the advertisement was more formal, involved in dressed-up elegance. Today, she has a more relaxed richness that reflects today's world. She's become less status-conscious. Our Estée Lauder woman is within reach. Her values and tastes change, she's interested in fewer objects that last forever. Although she's lovely, she may not wear only new clothes and her hair may not be letter-perfect. Karen Graham, who has represented us for years, has matured along with us, improved as we have, and still sells Estée Lauder with her look. We're not the sort of company that believes beauty belongs only to the very young. Shaun Casey and, more recently, Willow Bay have also appeared exclusively for us.

It took an artist to photograph the image we insisted upon—Victor Skrebneski of Chicago, the famous portraitist. His work is peerless. He has traveled worldwide to achieve just the right backgrounds for our campaigns. Whenever an advertisement comes out, we receive hundreds of letters and calls asking not about the cosmetics but about the featured jewelry and furniture. "Where'd you get the breakfront? That table?" "How much did that gold choker cost, and the vase—does it come in green?" There is actually a home in Palm Beach entirely furnished from our advertisements. The owner, herself, calls it the Estée House.

We had a model spokeswoman. Now, all we needed was a genius.

PACKAGING THE IMAGE

We found him. Ira Howard Levy is probably the most fertile mind in corporate design. He is able to interpret wishes and inspiration into the most creative and luxuriously beautiful wrappings, containers, boxes, papers. He has the talent to find the classical in both contemporary and ancient inspirations. He always does justice to the product.

I am what you would call a stern taskmaster. I expect perfection. And then a little more perfection when perfection is offered. Ira once said that I was like his grandmother when she made soup. She created the most perfect soup in the world, she used every extraordinary *and* ordinary ingredient in her bag of tricks, and when she finished a stellar soup, she threw in a little bit more.

At Estée Lauder, we all expect unrelenting, single-minded perfection.

We don't mind admitting that we are quality fanatics. Compromise is not in our vocabulary if the compromise affects the purity of the product in any way.

There may be some who say things about me that are less than flattering—that is to be expected with any public figure. Even detractors could never accuse me of being stupid or of penny pinching. I pay the best salaries anywhere for the best staff, just as I pay top dollar for the purest, finest, most effective ingredients and research. But I expect the best in return from my staff.

Ira was having a holiday. I will be charitable and not say that he vacationed as far away from me as he could manage. He found himself climbing a mountain in the Himalayas. A very high mountain. In New York an emergency demanded his attention.

Ira had just reached the air-thin top of the mountain, where sat a tiny hut, peopled by just one lonely Sherpa tribesman and a wireless phone to the earth. As my director of design approached the hut, weary and yearning for water and rest, the Sherpa emerged and said, "There's a phone call for you."

I found him. I always find him—or the person for whom I happen to be searching.

Ira Levy is one of the key men in our organization because packaging is a prime selling tool. When the R. J. Reynolds Tobacco Company, for example, decided in 1958 to upgrade its image and remove the picture of the camel from the cigarette pack, loyal Camel smokers were in an uproar. They thought the product had been changed as well—and it really hadn't been. The package is the product, say some, although I wouldn't, because I know better. Still, I know that orange juice tastes better from an orange carton than from a blue one. Lauder for Men in a stunning architecturally sound bottle will sell better than the same Lauder for Men in a plain, modest round bottle. I'll tell you why. A good part of beauty depends on self-image. If a man puts his after-shave lotion on from a solidly rippled, satisfying-in-the-hand bottle, an expensive-looking, masculine bottle, he stands taller, smells better, feels somehow *worthier*. Packaging design should be called packaging communications. You're telling someone about himself through the package. Of course, if the product is inferior, no bottle in the world will cause the customer to come back for more—or to stand tall.

We often change the look of popular items at holiday times. The customer recognizes old favorites and appreciates spruced-up packages. Until an item is well established, we'll maintain what we call product-package identity, so that customers will quickly be able to find their new favorites in the *expected* package.

At Estée Lauder, the designers work on the packages and product containers, then give their drawings to package development. These are the artists who make the inspiration a reality. Elaine Marstad is our resident genius in charge of package development. Her department's work dovetails with design development, forming a perfectly symbiotic relationship. One department cannot work without the other. It's team effort at its finest.

TRANSLATION

Translation is what packaging is all about. If I have an idea or find a piece of fabric that would be magnificent for a package, the design, packaging, and production departments turn the idea into reality. They translate ideas or raw materials into paper or metal for containers.

Walking on a beach in Florida one day, I found a perfect conch shell. I polished and polished it to bring out a pearly, opalescent quality. I knew that this object would contain a product one day. I carefully wrapped the shell and sent it by courier to my office. There the various departments of the packaging division made a nearly exact duplicate of the shell to hold a solid perfume. On anyone's coffee table, my container can rest proudly among other fine gold, silver, or enamel boxes. It is no less beautiful.

A Battersea box found in an antique store becomes another fragrance holder and a swatch of exquisite blue velour material from Italy becomes the pattern and color for the holiday Youth-Dew box. Once I found an ancient chatelaine, the chain from which the mistress of a castle would hang her scissors, keys, and purse, and this became the model for many perfume and makeup compacts interpreted in vermeil-like, gold-plated metal. A floral tile from Venice's San Marco Cathedral caught my eye, and the design department turned out boxes and paper in the same pattern. My mother's silver brush was the inspiration for a silver bottle top. I found a battered embroidered shawl with the most extraordinary needlework. Ira ignored the condition of the shawl and seized upon the handiwork, Elaine translated Ira's blueprints, and we had a magnificent paper! Cinnabar's wrapping paper came from the design of a pair of Evelyn's carved cinnabar earrings. We didn't know it at the time, but the design is an ancient Oriental symbol of good luck—a happy coincidence. Joe had a silk dressing gown whose design I knew would be perfect for the box for the cologne named after him—J·H·L. I sent to Paris for the last bolt of the fabric they had. Though simple, a unique black stripe graces every box—and makes it sell.

We must have tried over fifteen samples of green linen before we finally found just the right color for Aliage—a *green* perfume. The same careful attention to detail went into the creation of the bottle. We started with a Lucite bottle, then went to glass because we wanted to avoid the delicacy of crystal; the woman who wears Aliage is a sturdy, athletic, on-the-move woman, not a fragile woman.

PROMOTING THE PRODUCT

My dreams of being an actress and of basking in the limelight were never really banished from my consciousness. Several times a year I put on a show that has all the drama and excitement of a Broadway opening. At holiday time, especially, we launch a promotion, the purpose of which is to introduce new products and to stimulate excitement for the old ones. Christmas isn't merely a season for us: it represents, in smell, sight, and sound, an entire historical epoch. In the days preceding a new promotion, everything moves fast and furiously, there's a heightened sense of drama in the air, and everyone is tense with anticipation. This is how it works.

In promotional films, newspapers, and magazines, at parties and meetings, we announce to the world what's in store for them from Estée Lauder in a "theme" chosen by me and the design and packaging departments. One year we turned to the ancient art of the Orient, and designs were influenced by India, Japan, and Thailand. Another year, nineteenth-century England was the theme for our promotion. These promotions are not accomplished haphazardly. The year Venice was our inspiration, for instance, a team of researchers made two trips to that city to find the original sources for the bronzes, mellowed golds, fantasy rococo, that would serve as models for our packages. I'd fallen in love with Venice and was convinced that jewelry, art objects, and one-of-a-kind treasures would be marvelous translated into bottles, jars, compacts, and paper. For instance, I brought home an antique vinaigrette, which was a box used for holding vinegar or some aromatic to be inhaled to blot out the stench of the Grand Canal or plague-ridden corpses. The vinaigrettes became the inspiration for solid perfume holders. Red and gilt paper boxes, fresco-flowered compacts, Titian-red lipsticks, Venetian court colors, were the passwords of the season. An audiovisual presentation for customers, buyers, and salespeople featured Canaletto and Guardi paintings, gondolas galore, and shots of design from ancient Venetian archives. Ira walked on an inlaid design on one Venetian sidewalk, which inspired the shape of the label for the Youth-Dew package. A pattern from the endpaper of a dusty Venetian book was the basis for a roll of drawer paper. One theme throughout the promotion—one theme to sell new colors and fragrances!

The gilt-framed cosmetics display box, the audiovisual presentation, the advertisements that would run through the year, and the designs for the boxes, bottles, containers, and papers often take a year and a half in preparation. The summer of 1983 found us conducting research for Christmas of 1985. Throughout the year after a promotion is launched, everywhere, from Hohokus to Pasadena, elaborate theme tie-ins appear. Thus, the year of our Venetian theme, our counters were draped in burnt umber and Venetian colors and mannequins were dressed in ornate Venetian jewelry. The New York *Times* reported in a story about promotions that "at the same time Lauder was steeping itself in all things Venetian, the Elizabeth Arden team was boning up on Byzantium. Marc Rosen, vice president of package design and creative merchandising at Elizabeth Arden calls the closeness in theme a 'complete coincidence.' "

One year, B. Altman asked us to create a special international promotion. We arranged to set up six booths and asked beauty experts from Japan, France, China, Germany, and Ireland to send representatives to staff them. If an Altman customer wanted to find out how women in China applied their makeup, she could go to that Estée Lauder booth. Makeup secrets from each of the five countries were available to her in addition to the makeup secrets of America at a booth called America—Fashions in Faces. I know the world is so small. It was wonderful to make it even smaller at Estée Lauder.

Tuscany, a men's fragrance, will soon be launched by Aramis. The orangy, sunlit colors of the Tuscan landscape, the terra-cotta of the frescoes, the scenes of the local people going about their business, shots of ancient statuary and museum treasures, and the splendid rich burnt-almond hues of this part of the world will be the background of print and audiovisual productions as well as of the products themselves. This will be a stunning promotion.

We launch each product with a wonderful huge party.

I love parties. Last spring, my daughter-in-law Evelyn had a brilliant idea for launching Lauder for Men. We held a luncheon at the Helmsley

Palace in New York in honor of the "Handsomest Men in New York." The purpose of a launch party is to attract media attention, and we knew we would attract more publicity with interesting guests. How do you get the mayor, governors, assorted princes, counts, society-page luminaries, architects to attend? Tell them they're handsome.

It worked like a charm. Evelyn met one of our invitees on the street.

"Are you coming to the luncheon?" she asked.

"Well," he hedged, "my schedule is unbearably tight this week."

"Do try," she said smiling. "Only the handsomest men are invited, you know."

"Well, maybe I can change something around," he said.

He did. Andy Warhol, Jerry Zipkin, Ambassador Francis Kellogg, the photographer great Norman Parkinson, Ahmet Ertegun, famous lawyers, doctors, stage stars, hundreds of people who never attend these affairs came to this luncheon. What a launch! There were articles in newspapers and magazines all over the country—even the venerable *New Yorker* wrote a piece, and *New York* magazine's writer claimed to have bought two bottles of the fragrance.

The day following a launch, every store sells out the new line we've just introduced. We don't cheer wildly because we know this means little. The customers are not primarily responsible for cleaning our shelves. The competition is. *It* never fails. It takes some time before the real sales figures come in.

CHAPTER 10

WHAT I DIDN'T LEARN FROM BUSINESS SCHOOLS OR BOOKS

The schools and the books make it all seem so cut and dried. If you do this, you get this. Well, that's wrong. Just as a mother comes to know and work with her toddler, an executive comes to know the special vagaries and unique sensibilities of her business and of her own inner voice that tells the truth—if she listens hard enough. It's a delicate business, business is, and I never yet met anyone who learned her business from a book or school, just as I never met a mother who raised a wonderful child from a book. Each business person must find a style, that voice that grows clearer and louder with each success and failure. Observing your own and your competitor's successes and failures makes your inner business voice more sure and vivid.

These were, for example, some of my own observations: "Business is slow, business is dead," said the Wall Street wizards. So how do you grow in a slow, dead market? we asked ourselves. Simple. You take a share away from someone else by coming up with a better product. Aramis. Clinique. Night Repair. *New* concepts. Better products.

We observed, very carefully, the marketing of competitors. One major advertisement thrust ran a photograph of a handsome man holding a bunch of daisies; it was Revlon's Chaz man selling men's fragrance to men. Chaz did poorly. Why? Men like to smell good, but they don't like to think of themselves as prancing around with daisies in hand. Our fragrance advertisements would have to be less ethereal, more manly.

All around, during the acquisition binges of the 1970s, we saw business firms becoming conglomerates. There was pressure to do the same. The Lauder inner voices said no, stick to what you know best and don't change it lightly. Today, the same firms are spinning off the subsidiaries because they weakened instead of strengthened the original product.

The voice grows stronger with each success, each observed failure. All one has to do is listen—and watch.

Business is a magnificent obsession. I've never been bored a day in my life, partly because as a true business addict it's never been enough to have steady work; I had to love what I was doing. Love your career or else find another. Measure your success in dollars not degrees. Respect your product.

Am I offering you glittering generalities just as the books and schools do? No. There's not much difference between businesses, and certain basics apply to every business even if the products lie at different ends of the spectrum. Soup, glue, or beauty can all be packaged in jars, tubes, and bottles and vended like any other commodity. The big difference lies in the *vendor*—you, not the items to be vended. Even excellent glues, soups, and beauty products can die in the marketplace if the vendor isn't passionate and clever. Develop your style.

Our unique style has come from years of trial and error. Truths have emerged that work for us. Let me share them with you.

LAUDERISMS

• *Find the proper location.* In real estate, there are three things that matter: location, location, location. If you're in the retail business, the same holds true. The positioning of the counter is crucial. Walk into any large, exclusive department store in any city in the world and, if it carries Estée Lauder products, chances are the counter will be at the right of the entrance. Fifteen years ago, I stood at the door of Saks Fifth Avenue for one whole week and I watched women enter. Nine times out of ten, the first place their eyes would wander would be to the right. Not to the left. Not straight ahead. Notice as you enter a store—where do *your* eyes go first? I felt certain that a colorful, attractive counter positioned to the right would draw a woman before she went anywhere else in the store. Of course, we can't always choose our spot but we try to keep right.

Space counts also. I remember when Joe and I opened at the new Bonwit Teller store in Chicago. We were competing very bitterly with Revlon at the time. We'd chosen our counter and our space. The store was due to open in a short time. Charles Revson came in—with a tape measure. He carefully measured to see how much space we had and how much was allotted to him. We had a few inches more. We also had the right location. First, there was a distinct chill in the air. Then, he gave orders to the store's cosmetics buyer to remove our merchandise and put his in its place. The buyer was torn. Revson was a personal friend of Bonwit Teller's president. We were an excellent customer. The buyer threw her keys on the floor in a fury. "*I'm* not moving Estée Lauder!" she announced.

Joe called Leonard in Paris and woke him with the problem. Leonard rubbed the six-hour time difference out of his eyes and called our regional marketing director, Warner Byrum. He told him to chain himself to the counter if necessary, but under no circumstances was he to allow our counter to be moved. Our man, faithful to the end, stayed in the store all night, with the Revlon salesman hovering, ready to move us. By 11 P.M., the store buyer had given up in despair and gone home. The store president was nowhere to be found. Our Warner did not leave the counter all night.

In the morning, we opened where we belonged. Revlon was to the left.

It's not always so dramatic, thank goodness.

• *When you're angry, never put it in writing.* I learned that rule a long time ago. If you write it down, you can never take it back. The recipient has your furious letter to rankle him for the rest of his life. It's like carving your anger in stone. That makes implacable enemies. If you tell him face to face, eventually you'll both cool off. You can then always smooth things over, and the relationship is not lost forever.

• *You get more bees with honey.* Remember this. Even if your anger is justified, don't ever sever relationships, especially business relationships. Being pleasant even when you don't feel like it is best for business in the long run. For example, I was never comfortable pulling out of a store even if they treated us poorly. If I had a disagreement with an owner or a manager and decided to leave, do you think that the word in the industry would have it that *I* decided to pull out? It would not. Rumors would spread that my products were inferior or not selling, even if that was not the truth. The manager would make it known that I was asked to leave. Unpleasant business. You get more bees with honey.

• *Keep your own image straight in your mind.* From the beginning, I knew I wanted to sell the top-of-the-line, finest-quality products through the best outlets rather than through drugstores and discount stores. And so we have. We don't do dungarees, we don't do tablecloths. We do the best skin products available today, the best makeup and fragrance products. If I were to sell our cosmetics at discount stores, our sales would pick up for a brief time, and then decline dramatically. We are not a budget market, and we know it. The woman who buys the best (not always the most expensive, by the way) is reassured by finding the best where she expects it to be. Our credibility would be harmed if we cheapened our image.

• *Keep an eye on the competition.* It can't hurt. This doesn't mean copying them, as I've made clear. Being interested in other people's ideas for the purpose of saying, "We can do it better," is not copying. Innovation doesn't mean inventing the wheel each time; innovation can mean a whole new way of looking at old things. We have, for example, a room set aside for competitive products. We study these products closely; it would be foolish to wear blinders.

We use defensive means also. Shredders. We never keep memos. Leonard, for one, hates memos. He likes handwritten notes because he feels, as I do, that memos get copied or filed and end up, too often, in unfriendly hands. Handwritten notes are just from me to thee and generally get tossed out in the wastebasket when they've been read.

• *Divide and rule.* In the beginning, I felt that our great strength lay in the fact that I was a woman telling other women how to make themselves beautiful, as opposed to Revson telling women that he, as a man, knew what would make women desirable to men. After a while, I became convinced that strength had less to do with being a female or a male executive than with being an executive at heart. One had to be sure of herself—or at least act as if she was. An executive had to subscribe to the divide and rule theory. For me, that meant that I could divide authority and responsibility among the best staff I could find; but if they didn't produce, it was time to rule. I must admit I'm not terribly democratic in my business, and neither is my son Leonard. There is always one person on top who must be the final authority. That doesn't mean I don't have friends among my staff—I certainly do. Still, at the office, the name of the game is Lauder, imperial as that may sound. Running a business is rarely a matter of group vote.

• *Learn to say no.* Along with divide and rule comes saying no. Saying yes all the time stems from a childish desire to please and be loved all the time. Executives must say no to inferior products and ideas, no to those who seem to be making a mistake. Sometimes this is difficult and even the most intractable of executives, like me, can be swayed.

A brand-new line was ready to be born. Advisers told me that studies and polls and questionnaires had determined that Premier would be a great new name for a line of cosmetics. I hated it. Premier? That meant a "beginning" to me rather than "first," which was what my advisers had in mind. Still, everyone persuaded me in eloquent argument that Premier would, one day, be as famous as Clinique. Have you bought anything named Premier lately? Of course you haven't. The line died instantly.

• *Trust your instincts.* I've discovered that pondering "facts" and other people's judgments usually leads me down the wrong path. My first reaction is almost invariably the right one. My body, my mind, my heart, tell me yes or no, and I've learned to act on my visceral reaction. Our brains are really tiny computers that register millions of impressions, every day, and store them away for future use. When it's time to compile the impressions, we do so instinctively—and that's called common sense. Common sense, instinct—trust that part of yourself, whatever you call it.

• *Act tough.* I'm interested in the word "tough." I hear it said frequently that entrepreneurs and executives should be tough. ARE WOMEN TOUGH ENOUGH TO SUCCEED? blare headlines from a dozen magazines. Toughness, let me tell you, is not dependent on being crude or cruel. You can be feminine and tough. I love my femininity—as much as I rely on my toughness.

What others call tough, I call persistent. If you know you're correct, you must be firm and not bow to pressure. Too often women are taught as little girls that sweetness is more valuable than persistence or stubbornness. Little boys, on the other hand, are taught to win. Persistence and being tough make for success. I can't count the number of little plaques that Ronald has given out that read, IT CAN BE DONE. I agree. Anything can be done if you're certain it's right and you stay firm.

I have some weaknesses in the "toughness" arena. Although I deal with customers and my own staff by being feminine and assertive at the same time, I still feel bereft when someone leaves. I try to hide that

Here are the five women who've represented us as "The
Estée Lauder Woman."

Phyllis Connors

Victor Skrebneski

FOR THE MOST BELIEVABLY
NATURAL RADIANCE
OF A LIFETIME – ESTÉE LAUDER
CREATES NEW "YOUTH-SHEEN"
LIQUID AND POWDER

Nature couldn't give you a more enduring
young look. Now any woman—at any age—can
wear Youth-Sheen at any hour of the day
or night for a fresh, gleaming true-to-life sheen
that actually seems to radiate from within.
Estée Lauder formulated Youth-Sheen in a near-
weightless liquid that flows on over the
skin like the essence of light itself—and
in a miniature compact-ful of shimmering,
glimmering, sparkling powder to carry with
you all through the day. Wear Youth-Sheen
liquid or powder here-and-there over your
make-up—or use as a complete make-up itself for
a radiance that's dazzling as sunlight on water.
Wear Youth-Sheen every day—and capture the
glowing look of young good-health for a lifetime.

Estée Lauder

You spent all summer getting a tan. Now keep it— with <u>Go-Bronze</u> by Estée Lauder

Simply smooth on Estée Lauder's transparent gel over or under make-up. Go-Bronze helps to keep your tan alive-looking, July-golden and glowing. Why let your face fade away between summers? Treat your complexion to a sunny climate all year long with Go-Bronze. Formulated in four shades to give natural warmth to every skin tone:

Early Sun, Golden Sun, Deep Sun, plus one new shade—rich Bronze Glow. Each, $5.

Estée Lauder

▼ Karen Graham

Karen Harris ▲

All you need is one beautiful drop to know why Estée Lauder was keeping <u>Private Collection Perfume</u> for herself.

ESTĒE LAUDER

▲ Shawn Casey   Willow Bay ▼

Mr. and Mrs. Joseph Lauder.

My sons, Ronald and Leonard.

Christmas in Palm Beach.
Left to right: Joe, William,
Ronald, Aerin, Jo Carole,
Gary, Evelyn, Leonard and
I. This photograph was
taken in 1972; my grand-
daughter Jane had not yet
been born.

Leonard and Evelyn Lauder.

My grandaughters, Jane and Aerin, running on the beach.

A family looking toward the future: Ronald hugging Jane and Jo Carole holding Aerin.

A Horst portrait. Typically, I am surrounded by flowers, which I find a constant source of inspiration.

Joe is enveloped in the aura of quiet dignity which so became him.

This is the last photograph of all of us together. It was taken at William's 21st birthday party at the ''21'' Club in New York; the year was 1981. William is learning the retail trade and Gary is working at a financial institution in New York. Both young men, along with my granddaughters, prepare to continue the tradition. I am very proud of my family!

I love him so much. I think of him every day of my life.

At a masked ball in Venice, Princess Grace said she knew me by my smile. I said I knew her by her beautiful eyes. But, it was the Estée Lauder fragrance that really gave her away.

It was sad to receive a Christmas card from this wonderful family without their darling wife and mother, Grace de Monaco. *Left to right*: Caroline, Albert and Stephanie with their father, Prince Rainier, embracing them.

We posed for a photo promotion.

Costume parties allow me to be
my most fanciful self. Despite
Joe's protestations, I think he
secretly enjoyed them.

An Indian party.

A twenties party.

Joe and I in period costumes celebrating Monaco's 100th anniversary.

A masked ball.

Mort Kaye

"Be old-fashioned" was the theme here.

Bert and Richard Morgan

Lady Bird Johnson is a woman I admire: she juggled a very big job and still remained a devoted wife and mother. Her love for nature perfectly complemented her natural, charming manner. This was taken in Palm Beach on a friend's yacht.

Rose Kennedy is a matriarch and a true beauty. She's a wise and dear friend.

Pat and Richard Nixon and the ''almost'' ambassador to Luxembourg.

Courageous and gracious Betty Ford lent an air of candor and charm to "her" White House.

Vice-President George Bush and I enjoying a joke.

side, but I can never bear to be abandoned even if I know it's because I might have been too demanding. For the most part, no one knows that. Up until now anyway. For most women, for me anyway, a half-boudoir, half-boardroom image is the image that works best, and neither is stronger than the other.

• *Acknowledge your mistakes.* We all make mistakes. What we don't all do is acknowledge them. I've always found that it's best to cut your losses rather than to stick to a sinking ship. One of my big mistakes was artificial eyelashes. I always hated them, but I jumped on the bandwagon when every other company came out with them. They always looked false, never stayed on, just weren't pretty. We withdrew from the lash market almost as soon as we entered it. Instead, I instructed my chemists to come up with a fabulous mascara. They did.

Another mistake was trying to reach the teenage market. Teen cleanser, teen this, teen that. Teens simply were not our image, even though teens can surely benefit from our products.

A mistake I did not make was involving myself in hormone hoopla. Hormones on the skin can be dangerous business. My uncle taught me that many years ago. Because they are absorbed, they can have side effects that may not show up immediately, they can drastically alter the balance of natural estrogens and progesterones, and they can stimulate the growth of facial hair. Hormones do produce a temporary swelling of the skin, which smooths out wrinkles, but the effect is not worth the risk.

You're allowed to make a mistake. Once.

• *Write things down.* Your mother probably told you this. She's right. I do have a retentive memory, but I still forget something if it's not written down somewhere. Sometimes I awake in the middle of the night to jot down an inspiration, and I can't even read my handwriting in the morning. It comes back.

• *Hire the best people.* You can be the director of the company but you can't be there to direct all the time. You have to hire surrogate bosses, responsible, thinking people who are able to move fast, take risks, and make judgments that would be similar to yours. This is vital. Hire people who think as you do and treat them well. In our business, they are top priority. I've already mentioned many of our best surrogates. Here are some others:

Wonderful Vivian Behrens, who heads product development.

Capable John Chilton, who heads our United States factories.

Brilliant Joe Gubernick, who heads research and development (he's the scientist who discovered the precious ingredients in Night Repair).

Southern charmer Ida Stewart, who traveled the whole country with me to teach others to sell.

Clever Rebecca McGreevy, our public relations expert: Elizabeth Arden never forgave my personnel department for hiring Rebecca away from the Arden camp.

Saul Magram, our secretary and general counsel, whose legal guidance is invaluable.

Trust your surrogates, or else they can't be of service.

I think particularly of the assistant secretary of our company, Jeannine Bouillier; there isn't a family secret she hasn't heard—and kept.

• *Break down barriers.* Walls between people are not conducive to sales. Offerings of food have been breaking down barriers for centuries. I've been entertaining people and offering sustenance ever since those early days at my Fifty-third Street office when I served elegant luncheons on my tiny terrace. But, a note: entertainment does not always have to be luxurious. The intimacy and charm of a small business luncheon can be more effective than an elaborate dinner. Sometimes I even have picnics in my business dining room high over Central Park, complete with picnic baskets, wine, red-and-white checked napkins, cold chicken, French bread, apples, cheese and cookies. Informality can be a wonderful barrier breaker.

• *Give credit where credit is due.* Simply said: if you want loyalty and best effort, you must be thoughtful. Have your actions speak eloquently to thank those who work for you. Everyone appreciates tokens of appreciation. Remember birthdays. Remember holidays. Your personal touch, your anniversary card will be received with happy thoughts of the sender.

Every Christmas, the Lauder family sends baskets of grapefruits or oranges to every single factory worker in our employ along with specially designed cards (that have been affectionately dubbed the grapefruit card): we try to send the spirit of the Florida sun even if we can't provide a Florida vacation for every worker! I derive great pleasure from giving, and those who are recognized feel wonderful.

• *Train the best sales force.* Executives need super-sales forces, trained according to their own specific needs. We train our people to sell in our own way. Yearly sales conferences are held, but *not* in large and exciting cities where trainees yearn to miss lectures to go shopping, to the theater, or to the latest art exhibition. They're held in out-of-town, rather remote spots, where the conference *is* the big show; in fact, the only show in town. We pepper our training sessions with delightful luncheons and in-house entertainment at night, to make them pleasurable experiences, but no one is mistaken: the object of the conference is selling techniques, *our* techniques.

Beauty advisers are trained to chart each customer's skin type, lifestyle, and product preferences. Each adviser has a sound background in skin care, so she can explain the differences between treatment, cosmetic, and fragrance products. I always give impassioned lectures to teach others how to sell afresh what they've sold a thousand times before.

There are always several options for customers who are invited to try new colors and products. No one is ever pressed by a hard and heavy sales technique. Customers are encouraged to buy only what they need and will use. I have a suggestion for the hiring executive: if you are searching for salespeople, and your business is related to beauty, don't hire a woman who smokes. It may sound sexist, but men are somehow allowed to smell of tobacco and women are not. If you're selling beauty, you must smell sweet.

THE ESTÉE LAUDER SALES MEETING

An Estée Lauder sales meeting is unlike any other sales meeting of any other business anywhere. Our sales meetings set the standard for the presentation of our products all over the world, and as such, they must be extraordinary. I have an uncompromising sense of detail which permeates everything I do. The meals I serve, the parties I have, the business I created, the places I go, my friends, my family, my business associates—everything must be treated with infinite respect and care. At a gathering of executives, I will invest the same sense of order, creativity, and energy as I would at a party in my home for personal friends or family. Consequently, the sales meetings at which I deliver the Estée Lauder message to those who must then go out and convey the same message to the customer are examples of high drama, compelling theater, and, finally, hard facts. We could get up and *tell* our salespeople "this is what we have to sell and go out and sell it" or we could *show* our salespeople what we have to sell and the manner in which we expect them to sell it. We choose the latter approach.

Let me give you an example. Recently we had a sales meeting to begin the promotion of the fragrance Beautiful. It was held at the elegant Pré-Catelan restaurant in Paris, and top executives, sales people, press, everyone right down to the men and women who will sell behind the counters in that area were invited. I visualize the new fragrance as a *pink*, beautifully pink fragrance and so the sales meeting was infused with pink. Traditionally, sales meetings take two days. The first day is festive. We had a pavilion built at the restaurant, an octagonal tent copied from an eighteenth-century tent in Versailles, and we laid a pink carpet from outside in the street into the dining area. My design department swept through Paris to buy up almost every pink flower that existed, and pink was out of season. Nevertheless, we found pink; some florists had only one or two fresh pink flowers. We bought them. We ransacked the city until we had enough pink flowers to fill our dining room with colored scent. Napkins were dyed the same soft pink as the Beautiful package, and so were tablecloths and tassels that adorned gifts of fragrance. I even wore a pink dress. The evening was breathtakingly pink and beautiful sounds, smells, tastes, and sense of the fragrance were passed along to the people who will sell. Everything was just right—just the right tablecloths, salt cellars, vases, flowers. I spoke with passion to the assembled, and so did other members of my family.

If I happen not to be available for a sales meeting, complicated hookups of phones are arranged, and from wherever I am, I speak to the group to tell them what a superb product we have, to tell them that I expect them to invest all *their* sense of passion and verve when they go out to sell. There are entertainments and the air is filled with elegance and a sense of festivity. Music is everywhere. So are fragrance and delicious tastes. Everything is perfect. Only by making it perfect for my own people will I be able to pass on the message that they must spend as much attention on detail as I do. They will pick up the thread of what I want by being treated with excellence.

Day two of the sales meeting is pragmatic. Leonard Lauder presides and hard numbers are discussed. When our people walk into the business meeting, they are wearing the scarves they've received as gifts the night before, humming the tunes they heard the night before, smelling the fragrance of the night before. When they walk into the business meeting to learn what and how they have to sell, they're halfway to success, already. They've subliminally picked up the Estée Lauder signals.

When our top executives go into the field to see store presidents or buyers in the weeks that follow, they reproduce the sales meeting on smaller scales but with no less attention to detail. Business breakfasts or luncheons are organized using the same pink cloths, the same napkins from our sales meeting after the linens are carefully laundered by a special laundress. In Dallas, Los Angeles, Tokyo, Milan, Palm Beach, and Athens, our sales people re-create the spectacular event they experienced at Pré-Catelan in Paris, with the same *peau de soie* tablecloth and the same pink napkins and fresh pink flowers and the spirit of the message is passed along.

All this sells creams. All this sells fragrance. We give theater and quality to our associates and customer. And the customer responds.

Some time ago, Leonard gave a wonderful speech to a select audience of businesswomen in which he summarized some of his thoughts about the growth of Estée Lauder. I would like to share them with you.

Keep a low profile, said my son, until you're large enough to compete seriously. If you're going into your own business or if you're already in a small business, don't disclose your sales and profits to anyone—either to brag or complain. This invites competitors to compete with you. Stay quiet until you're strong enough to be unmistakably visible.

Think small, he told the rapt audience. Thinking small brings big profits. You can do anything if you're small enough. Conventional wisdom says the bigger you are, the more profitable and efficient you are. We disagree. We break down each of our manufacturing units all around the world into smaller, manageable groups so the directors of each can guide by reaching out, knowing everyone's strengths and weaknesses, and "touching" the personality in each person who works. This goes back to my original theory that once you touch a woman's face, you have her. Thinking small even applies to the number of customers a business tries to reach. We'd rather aim for several great department stores who love us rather than thousands of tiny buyers who are not committed to our product.

Be your own boss—stay private! said my son.

If we had to please investors, we'd have stringent financial controls, we'd have to explain and justify every decision. That would be bad business for people who rely on strong feelings about what's right rather than on black and white "facts," which often turn out to be false. If you're your own boss, you can move fast. When ideas have to be implemented overnight, speed, flexibility, and authority to make decisions without consulting shareholders are of utmost importance. As a family business, we can also invest in research and development and go ahead with a product *or* call a halt to it. I can't tell you how many batches of perfume or creams I've ordered discarded because they weren't exactly right. Re-Nutriv, for example. The hand samples, the small test batches of just five pounds weight, seemed fine. When one hundred pounds of cream were produced and put into jars, something had gone wrong. The whole hundred pounds had to be discarded even though no one but I would have known the difference.

Quality first, sales later. We keep perfect samples of all our creams and fragrances and always test new batches against them to see that the quality remains consistent. We try them in the heat of the sun and in the cool of air-conditioned rooms, and whatever is not perfect is thrown out. No votes are taken. Try doing that with a thousand shareholders looking over your shoulder.

I had lunch with Bernard Gimbel after he went public. "Don't do it, Estée," he urged. "I travel second class now because I have to make a report for everything!"

Visualize, said Leonard to the businesswomen. He meant it quite literally. I know, as he does, that one can will oneself to success. If in your mind's eye you see a successful venture, a deal made, a profit accomplished, it has a superb chance of actually happening. Projecting your mind into a successful situation is the most powerful means to achieve goals. If you spend time with pictures of failure in your mind, you will orchestrate failure. Countless times, before the event, I have pictured a heroic sale to a large department store every step of the way and the picture in my mind became a reality. I've visualized success, then created the reality from the image. Great athletes, business people, inventors, and achievers from all walks of life seem to know this secret. Norman Cousins, the writer, was once told he had a fatal illness. He absolutely refused to accept the diagnosis! Instead, he visualized himself well and happy, and made the mind picture a reality.

And then, Leonard concluded in his comments, it takes a thief to catch a thief. The most formidable competitor that you can conjure up is yourself. Aramis for men competes with Clinique for men, which competes with the newest products, Lauder for Men. Every company within Estée Lauder can compete with one another because we're the best judge of our own weaknesses, gaps, and strengths. Various companies within the original company are geared to divergent public needs. This practice never cannibalizes the parent company but only invigorates it.

Our ideas, I wish to make clear, are not meant to be the guideposts of your business. Just as I did not learn my business from a book or school, I'm sure you shouldn't accept everything said in this book as gospel. Still, it can't hurt to have an open mind about what works and what doesn't work for others. You must cull only the relevant matter for yourself from everything you read or hear.

These thoughts are the cornerstone of business for the Lauders. If they're not complicated or scholarly, they have the advantage of effectiveness. They've worked for us. Big business, I think, is a combination of timing, hard work, and an ability to see beyond one's nose. Patience. People with big ideas and dreams often fail because they can't wait out the slow times.

Finally: the same principles that contribute to business success apply equally to women as they do to men. Business doesn't have a sex. Demand the finest quality in product and performance. Tell your story with enthusiasm. Always look for things that should be changed. We learn too much, every day, to be satisfied with yesterday's achievements.

Sometimes, I have to pinch myself to believe what hard work and prayer have brought me. They've taken me from carrying a tiny bottle of cream in my purse on the off chance I'd meet a woman who needed a quick lift of glow to seeing a streamlined white streak as I drive along the Long Island Expressway, thirty-three miles due east of Manhattan. The streak is my factory, and as my car approaches, my name gets larger and larger. It is a thrill that will never diminish for me. My name, not in lights, as the little girl from Corona dreaming of being an actress hoped to see, but my name on a working monument to beauty.

PART THREE

LIVING
THE DREAM

CHAPTER 11

LIVING WELL
AND LOVING IT
(PEOPLE, PARTIES, AND PLACES
I HAVE KNOWN)

Too many people mark time instead of living their lives. They count their problems instead of their joys, and their days pass, sodden and eventless. I've always found that sad and frustrating to observe. Just as one can always make business when others say there is none, one can always make fun when all around is somber and dull. I cherish each moment. Working hard and living well are taking full advantage of one's time.

Living well should not be an embarrassment. It's great, good fun, and it's very nourishing to enjoy the fruits of one's labor. There is no denying that it's fine to be financially comfortable. This is not to say that it's terrible to be poor. I know many life-affirming people without a great deal of money who have infinite sources of satisfaction. There is an art to living well, and wealthy people don't have a monopoly on that. In fact, the lack of financial means often spurs one's imagination to greater heights of good living. I have experienced lean times. That's why I worked so hard to achieve what I do have. If I had not met with financial success, I know my life would have been joyful anyway. I would have *made* it so.

Still, given my predilection for the good life, I'll take the intense work *and* the intense pleasure that comes from hard-earned compensation. This is not always as simple to accomplish as it may seem. There are women with a great deal of money who are stingy, not only with their dollars, but with their nice times as well. These are the same women who ration out perfume in tiny, select dabs instead of applying it lavishly and giving themselves generously to a rich aura of fragrant life.

I know there are those who criticize luxury, implying that as long as hunger and war exist anywhere, behavior should be appropriately solemn. I must take exception to that kind of thinking. It's life-destroying. Certainly, one has to pay dues, pay a great deal for the privilege of living in a sweet world and for the great, good fortune of being successful. I give as much as I can to alleviate sadness, hunger, and lack of hope. I make contributions to promote education—the greatest way out of despair—and I give time and effort, the kind of effort I put toward my business and life. Having done that, I can't believe that rewarding one's own hard work with glamour and excitement is profligate. I don't want to miss any part of life, and living well is certainly one of the better parts.

Along with the best things in life that are free, I adore the best things in life that come dear. I love the sheen of a richly dark, mahogany table polished to diamond-bright brilliance. I love the look of a ruby strawberry, floating in champagne bubbles in a crystal goblet.

I love the feel of a liquid-silk ball gown. I do love pretty clothes.

A PASSION FOR FASHION

There are many who turn up their noses at the very idea of fashion. They often dress "antifashion," and that, of course, is just as fashionable among their peers as my kind of fashion. What is my kind of fashion? I admire a dress that's been wonderfully cut in the richest, loveliest fabric. Although fashion often begins with the young people in the street who are daringly imaginative, for me it originates in the great couturier houses in Paris and Milan. *Haute couture* establishes a standard. Much of what is seen in the stores in the year following the semiannual shows reflects variations of the styles of the great dress designers' collections. Their shows are attended by the editors of the fashion magazines, the presidents and buyers of the best stores, the actresses, princesses, and socialites who admire a particular designer, and people like me, who come for inspiration as well as to buy. While the fashion buyers are eager to see new silhouettes, trends, and hem lengths, I look for new colors and new fashions for faces.

I always go to a fashion show on the first day, and I always sit in the front row, the most prized row of seats. And I learn. One year, at an Ungaro show, I was mesmerized by one model who had the palest skin. She wore the most exquisite shade or ruby-red shadow on her lids. It looked stunning—that pale translucent skin, the red lips, the romantic, mysterious eyes. I couldn't wait to get home to experiment until I found exactly that color for our own shadows. Fashions in faces— I find them everywhere and I especially find them at the shows. At the Yves St. Laurent show, I came away with the brilliant idea of huge, oversized scarves. His models wore them thrown casually on one shoulder with many wonderful outfits. For me, that was the fashion tip of the season. A woman could change her whole look or the look of an old dress simply by wearing a beautiful scarf in this striking way. I also learned another thing by watching the models at various shows: an all-in-one-color look makes one appear taller, leaner. A model who may wear a natural beige satin suit will wear beige shoes and beige stockings so as not to "break the line."

It's not necessary to go to fashion shows to learn. Anyone can read *Vogue, Harper's Bazaar, Town and Country,* or some other wonderful fashion magazine and pick up the tricks of the trade by studying the way models are "put together." For instance, by reading a magazine you might discover that purple and red is a divine combination or that veils give a sense of allure and mystery to almost anyone. I must confess, I wear veils even when they are not ordained "in style."

I believe in buying fewer clothes, but good ones. If something goes out of fashion or if hemlines change, I just put my good dresses away for a few seasons—and pull them out again when they return to high style, as they invariably do. As the saying goes, "Everything old is new again . . ." And when it comes to fashion, that is certainly true.

A word about styles. It's never a good idea to dress lavishly according to the latest word from the latest designer. It's always so much better to keep in mind what looks good on you and adapt the latest style accordingly. I have an almost nonexistent waistline and thus never wear clothes with waistlines no matter who says they are in. I may adapt and wear what's stylish around my face and neck, but never will I wear a dress that's fitted at the waist.

There's glamour in fashion, but there's also practicality. It's practical to look your prettiest and feel your best and thus be ready to take on the world. Practical women don't have to look like hausfraus in cotton dresses. I'm quite practical, but I love pretty and well-designed clothes that make me feel finished.

Princess Grace once told me that as a child she felt so "bland" she almost crawled into the woodwork. It's hard to imagine the young Grace Kelly being insecure about the impression she made on others, but it's easy to understand how all this changed when she discovered makeup and fashion. Her natural beauty came alive with energy and style when she learned how to enhance it with color and flair.

SETTINGS

An emerald placed in a simple setting is quite a different ring from an emerald placed in an ornate setting. Settings (or environments) influence people as strongly. When I find myself in a new and fresh milieu, all my senses become enriched and sharper. Creativity, after all, is nothing more than the sharpening of every sense. In the process of creating new fragrances and colors, I constantly call upon my sight, my taste, my hearing, my "nose" to tell me "Yes, this is wonderful!" or "No, this is not quite wonderful enough."

Different countries serve as splendid settings. Each country has a different cuisine, different music, different dress. Some are sultry and sensual. Some are lighthearted and gay. To create a great fragrance, one must be aware of the sounds and smells and tastes of many settings and one sense feeds another. Different parts of the world trigger new ideas and images, and for me, invention depends on a kaleidoscope of changes.

By living in different places throughout the seasons, I am able to breathe in these varying influences and essences. It wouldn't be the same if I were just a tourist and stayed a few days at a hotel; I need to call these different settings all over the world *home*. I need to be part of the landscape and the air and the light of varying countries.

I decided to exchange my concept of home by buying property in different parts of the globe. Now, I could always be at home even when I was away from home.

All my residences have one thing in common—a sense of airiness, lightness, and brightness. Although they look quite different from one another, they share this enlivening quality.

HOME SWEET HOMES

My first residence abroad became a wonderful reality after a holiday in the south of France. The thought of leaving this beautiful part of the world was dispiriting. I told Joe that I dearly wished we owned a home in this sparkling spot.

"Let's buy one," Joe said with a smile. A little encouragement was all I needed. I called Mercury Real Estate at the Hotel Carleton, and an agent took us out that very day to see an immaculately clean and charmingly intimate house. I took out what francs I had in my purse, Joe emptied his pockets and we made a down payment on a new setting.

My home in France faces Italy. The rooms are small in the provincial style. I can see the boats bobbing on the turquoise Mediterranean from my bedroom window. The ambience is wonderfully inspiring. When I watch the curtains billow in the soft, fragrant breeze, I am moved to transfer that quality of sweetness to the scents I create so naturally there. The house is set high on a graceful half-round terrace that gives the sense of rising loftily above the whole city of Cannes. My Gallic garden is magnificent and very much in the style of the famed English gardens because it has an abundance—thousands and thousands—of blooms. Being surrounded by color and fragrance is as important to me as eating. Just recently, when I was working on our new fragrance, Beautiful, I went, for inspiration, to visit the fabled gardens at Giverny where Monet created his art. I was gratified to note that my own French garden is as breathtakingly similar in variety, if not in size, to the Giverny master-piece.

Since I see fragrance, my whole life is rooted in the visual. When I find myself surrounded by the misty spires of London, I love to visit the famous English formal gardens outside of the city. There's not an abundance of sunshine in London, as you'd imagine, and yet, when I'm at my English residence, I still need to gaze out at an enchanting, idyllic vista of fragrant flowers: I need it for my work and I need it for my spirit! The London garden is alive with white—creamy whites, frosty whites, silvery whites, marble whites, fleecy whites. Every crack be-tween every stone is blooming with white tulips, rhododendron, aza-leas, or lilies. Whenever I am here, I feel drenched with the sweetest of auras.

The flat in London, on an elegant eighteenth-century square, is fur-nished with English Sheraton and Chippendale furniture that I brought from America! The wonderfully hand-carved pieces were transported to the United States by some of the great American families around the turn of the century. It pleases me to have returned these beautiful pieces to the land of their origin.

Aliage, my sports fragrance, was created around the time I bought my home in London. Since it was inspired by the look and scent of a palm leaf, I had green on my mind when I was searching for just the right shade for my sitting room. An ancient celadon vase was the source for the special green I finally chose. My English bedroom is papered with a striking blue and white design that just happens to be the wallpaper that Thomas Jefferson used at Monticello so I have bits of my American heritage in Britain.

In Florida, the breezes of the Atlantic invigorate my senses and it is there that I love to look at the winter packagings that my design department is planning for Christmas. My home in Florida is open and airy and the clarity of the light is exquisite. I know that if the wintery Christmas colors work in Florida, they will work in Chicago in December. This is an important concept in my work. I get ideas for packaging, as well as for products, in the different atmospheres of my homes. Somehow, when I choose a crystal bottle for a fragrance, the vibrant sensuality of the Parisian streets where the tradition of fine crystal is legendary helps me to make the correct choice. I can be confident that a brilliantly faceted crystal container chosen in Paris will look glorious in New Jersey, Colorado, or Copenhagen.

Lately, the delicate and ordered charm of an early, more rural America has captured my imagination. I find my way to the American countryside where a lovely walk in the country, or a Sunday exploration of local antique shops, yields a piece of fabric here, an antique silver box there, a bibelot or a faded painting that will turn out to be the inspiration of a package design. Ever since I saw *Gone With the Wind*, I always wanted to have a picturesque house with white Corinthian columns. I found such a place nestled in the rolling hills of Long Island, not far from New York City. Here I escape to rest and be alone with nature and sometimes to search for American folk art with which I've recently come to be enchanted. In fact, right now, we're currently exploring ways to present Aliage in nineteenth-century Americana design just because my home in the American country means so much to me.

My homes, in every sense of the word then, are settings of inspiration. Living in different environments throughout the year enables me to revitalize my creative "juices." The rhythm of my year, the shape of my travels changes in response to what I need to do in my business. I don't move from country to country, house to house to follow a preordained social calendar; I move to seek new ideas and directions. When a color or a fragrance calls for the breezes off the Atlantic, I set my sights for that area. When I sense that the foggy elegance of London would be right for the colors that are being born in my factory, I go there to work. Different homes in different settings act as places in which to take refuge from the whirl of business and sociability, and they also act as the very founts of inspiration. They refresh me in every way.

THE SOCIAL WHIRL

When I'm working, and when I'm playing, I'm happiest to be with interesting and shining personalities. People are my fuel and my fun— they charge me with energy and excitement, and give me great pleasure. My year is filled with business activities that encompass a vast network of friends, dining out, and parties. Each feeds into the other and enriches the other, and all this happens in every corner of the world, where I travel to touch base with people and business developments.

The camaraderie of a luncheon, for instance, is an international event. A luncheon within the setting of a famous, busy, great restaurant has great drama and appeal. In New York, I meet those I've seen or read about the night before at Le Cirque, La Grenouille, or La Côte Basque for luncheon. The "right" table at every restaurant is the place where one can see and be seen as others enter and I love to greet both business and social acquaintances from the "right" table and not from "Siberia," as the less prominent tables are called. On Sunday afternoons in New York, Mortimer's is the place to people-watch for the international set, and I look forward to the pleasant conversation I know I'll share with my luncheon companions. In Paris, look for me at Maxim's, Le Relais, at the Plaza Athénée, and in London, at Harry's Bar, Mark's, or Claridges. I delight in greeting friends and enjoying extraordinary gourmet meals. In a special way, I find it comforting as well—it always makes me feel "at home" when I'm on the move on business. Seeing familiar faces in unfamiliar places gives one a sense of roots.

Somehow, I never tire of wonderful parties either—if they are truly wonderful. They whet the imagination, encourage me to dress up and look my loveliest, and bring me into the world.

I tend to work nonstop during the day, usually seven days a week. I'd be a one-song woman, a one-note friend if that's all I did. If I stayed home, what would I see? Going out (I have to admit, about five times a week is my average) widens my horizons and gives me two ways of life.

It does something else as well. It helps business. It keeps me in touch with the people who buy and sell my cosmetics. It keeps my finger on the pulse of my customers, who are also the kind of people I choose as friends. How would I know which fragrance women really love if I didn't smell it on them?

I go out to see what people look like to get ideas for faces and fragrances. It's very useful to stay in close social contact with business associates. Those who are connected with my business life—store owners, buyers, media people, movie stars, countesses, young career women—are involved on another level in my social life. Since night and day selves differ, we all can see multiple facets of one another at parties. If we share some fine conversation and wine, we get to know and like one another more. It is often quite a practical matter. It does no harm for a serious businessperson to hobnob with the great, the near great, and the merely fascinating. As Oscar Wilde sagely observed, "To be in society may be a bore, but to be out of it is a disaster.'' My experience has been that it's rarely a bore.

Sometimes people ask me, ''What do you talk about at these formal parties?''

The answer is everything . . . and nothing. Inevitably, on one side of me at dinner there'll be a gentleman who will say, ''Tell me how you got started.''

''When you finish dining, we'll talk about it a little, and someday I'll write a book and talk about it a lot,'' has been the answer up until now.

My social life reaches out to the heart of the place I'm visiting. In London, there are the races at Ascot or the matches at Wimbledon or the polo games that are so much fun. With the unforgettably radiant Princess Diana, I watch her handsome husband, Prince Charles, lead his team to victory. In Milan, the opera is heart-stoppingly beautiful and so are the Italian women, who dress with such glory and grand style. In every city, there's the theater, the music, the food, that make it unique, and with friends and family, I thrill at being a citizen of the world.

I am constantly on the move, and I travel with so much luggage it's embarrassing. I never have matched luggage, so no one knows instantly which pieces are mine. Some new suitcases, some old, some even with covers, come rolling around the luggage trolley when I get to town, but all my luggage is marked with a distinguishing sign, like a red or blue ribbon, so I can identify what's mine. When in doubt, while packing, I always think, Take more! In the fall I always take a red velvet hat— that, above all, is the one item for which I've found infinite use.

In my own beloved country, there are wonderful parties and won- derful people as well. Perhaps nowhere else does the international set come together so vividly. In Palm Beach, Marjorie Merriweather Post gave some perfectly grand parties. She would transport eminent guests from all over the world in her private plane. I love the Red Cross Ball, which is given annually in Palm Beach—there may be nothing in the world quite so thrilling as hearing the Marine Corps singing "The Star-spangled Banner" to an assembled group of gloriously gowned and tuxedoed people in a party mood.

There is no doubt about it—I am a social animal. For sheer entertainment value, let me be with friends who just happen to be among the movers and shakers of the world. There is nothing more exhilarating.

COME TO MY PARTY

Going to wonderful parties is a celebration. But having a wonderful party is a gift you give to friends. It's an expression of self, a message that says I want you to have a good time in my home and I want to share my love and my best efforts with you . . . because you mean so much to me. Whether it's a holiday party with family or a formal dinner party for a head of state, a party, given with style and thought, is one of life's joys. Think what you offer your guests—beauty, conversation, new ideas, and the most memorable dining experiences (you hope) of a lifetime. A dinner party is pure theater—the setting of the table, the guest list, the choreography of the cocktail hour. A party should have elements of high drama in the beauty of the scene, the finest of music and the exciting play of wonderful clothes. Need I tell you that I love dressing up for a party? Why waste the gathering of friends on everyday clothes? It's so much more entertaining to preen one's feathers! So much more fun!

I love to entertain in the grand manner. I invest more time and diligence in an effort to present the perfect evening than most people invest in planning their daughter's wedding. If you do anything, do it right.

FANTASTIC FÊTES

Doing it right, for me, extends every few years to a party that wholly challenges my sense of drama and grand scope. Periodically, I have a need to see *lots* of people dancing, gasping with pleasure, enjoying life! The moods usually come when I'm impelled to share a wonderful idea or happening with others, and over the years, some of my very, very special parties have been prompted by an historic or artistic revelation. Let me give you an example:

About six months before the Pablo Picasso show came to the Museum of Modern Art in New York, I began to realize that this show would change the sensibilities of the American public—that's how important it was. Never before in history had so many Picassos been in one place at the same time. I knew the exhibit would influence colors, fashion, fragrance and artistic consciousness for a very long time afterwards. I loved Picasso. I had seen many of his less famous but magnificent paintings and sculpture in Paris, in London, in a tiny house of his friend in the south of France near where the great artist had lived. I felt the exhibition at the museum would be an event of great significance. I wanted to introduce him to my special friends and business acquaintances in my own way.

Invitations were sent to hundreds of extraordinary people all over the world. They were to come to a Picasso party that would be held in the great dining room of the Museum of Modern Art. I arranged my decor. Tablecloths were ordered on which paintbrush strokes in the colors Picasso used during his Cubist period were splashed; marigold yellows, the strong pink of impatiens, the blue of the Côte d'Azur became the setting for dinner plates. Napkins were dyed a vibrant terra-cotta—the color of Picasso's painted rooftops of the French villages—and on each napkin, his signature in a beautiful, cool white. The napkins would serve as mementos of the evening for my treasured guests. Centerpieces at each table were terra-cotta vases, which we had carefully reproduced in the style of the ceramics Picasso created; filling the vases were wildflowers we had flown in from France—the orange day lilies, the French Queen Anne's lace, the mimosa that had surrounded the artist as he worked. When you entered the dining room in New York at the museum, the scent was the same that entranced Picasso as he looked out at his gardens from his terrace.

I worked closely with the chefs to make sure the menu was one Picasso would have loved if he were a guest, and the milk-fed spring lamb, the fresh Dover sole flown in from the English Channel, the Brie, cooked *en croûte*, succulent and crispy at once, the cool, light-as-a-feather coffee soufflé were his favorites and were divine. Picasso's presence permeated the atmosphere in subtle and lovely ways. After dinner, the museum was opened to my guests and, in their beautiful clothes, they drifted through the galleries. Guitarists softly played the flamenco music Picasso listened to as he created the very paintings we were looking at. If ever I longed for my days of drama as a very young actress, that evening satisfied all such yearnings. As each guest left, he received a beautifully bound catalog of the historic Picasso exhibit. Each book was engraved with the name of a guest. In all modesty, I think no one will ever forget that party, and even today, I feel thrilled as I remember its beauty and poignancy.

To introduce our Venetian colors to our sales forces, I planned a party in Florida that would bring the color, sound and excitement of Venice to my business associates. The food was designed to taste of Venice, and the golden and red menus told my guests they would be eating Tortellini San Marco, Vitello alla Veneziana with Pesto Sauce, arugula-endive salad, frozen zabaglione with fresh berries and other Italian delights. A wandering minstrel serenaded the tables in Italian. The high drama came as my guests left. We'd wired speakers into the palm fronds and, a few feet from my friends, an extraordinary display of fireworks was set off and keyed to the cadence of the rousing music of Vivaldi's *Four Seasons*. My friends just stared in delighted amazement, unable to believe the extravaganza in front of them.

For these spectacular parties, I've always had a special fondness for Valentine's Day because it is the holiday of love and affection. Joe and I usually gave a party on this day. I remember February 14, 1980, with special joy. I wanted to create menus that people would keep and cherish with pleasure as I've saved menus from special evenings. After searching for just the right thing for weeks, I finally found, in a tiny antique store in Manhattan, a wonderful collection of Victorian valentines, each different and each printed between 1880 and 1890. On the inner leaf of each menu, I affixed one of these exquisite valentines: you could almost hear the courtly exchange of the long-ago lovers who first received the lacy, charming cards. The menu was printed in careful calligraphy on the facing leaf and we wrapped the outside of the menu in the brightest, reddest crepe de Chine material we could find. The finished product looked more like a love offering than a dinner menu. It was so pretty!

On the table, I remember, I placed tall, graceful cylinders of clear crystal and filled them with flowering white quince, which had been wrapped in packages of dry ice and flown in from South Carolina, and besides the quince, there were cylinders of crimson amaryllis and fragrant white lilacs. What a table . . . it was spectacular.

Speaking of tables, I might add that it is of utmost importance when giving a large party with many tables that the guests move to the dining room in a smooth, choreographed entrance. Nothing puts a damper on those first few moments more than guests who must search clumsily for their seats. I have always disliked numbered tables—they are so cold and impersonal. Sometimes, to assist the smooth flow, attractive young women, dressed in clothing that complements the party motif, show guests to their seats. Sometimes I differentiate tables by different symbols or names of flowers or countries—or even just colors, a red table, a gold table, a green table . . . The year of the Valentine Day's party I mentioned, we had great Lucite hearts of different colors—white, pink, red, and silver to mark tables—and when each guest picked up his or her place card at the entrance to the dining room, the card showed a heart in the color of the heart at her special table.

One of my favorite events has always been the annual Christmas party I give for the people who work for me. I'm so grateful to them, especially the salespeople who spend every day with my products. If it weren't for them, I wouldn't be me, and I know it. It's business that gave me what I have, and that is never forgotten. Through business, I have met an infinite variety of fascinating people, and I have been entertained royally by so many, I like to respond in kind.

HE GAVE UP HIS KINGDOM FOR
THE LOVE OF A WOMAN

One couple who entertained us royally was the Duke and Duchess of Windsor. I fell into the pleasant habit of giving the Duke and Duchess an anniversary party each June, and every year the Duke would say to me, "We'll see you next year at this same time Estée."

At such parties, we always presented the Duchess with a list of all those to be invited—she always liked to know who would be where she would be. She had a problem with numbers that always had to be overcome: a strong superstition precluded her dining where there would be just thirteen people present. That meant the Duchess was not happy if fourteen or eleven people were planned for. One guest not showing up would bring the party to thirteen in the former case, and two extra that the hostess might invite at the last minute could too easily bring a party of eleven to thirteen. I told her in the beginning of our relationship that since my dinner table needed a minimum of eighteen to be well apportioned, we didn't have a problem. Our parties together usually involved twenty-two or twenty-four people, including people she had suggested and my own intimates, none of whom ever have canceled for that dinner, no matter who came to town unexpectedly.

The Duke himself made no requests—just appeared with his wife. I always sensed a quietness in this gentle, sad-eyed man, a homesickness of which he never spoke but which just seemed to cling to him. He had had a German nurse, and much of his childhood was spent in

Vienna, where he went to school. He spoke to me in fluent German as we shared our memories of the place my own mother loved and the place to which I had returned with so much pleasure year after year. We both relished the warmth and lilt of Viennese music. The Duke told me that he had always, as a boy, slipped the court musicians a few coins to play his favorite songs over and over. The musicians in his father's court always complied. Naturally they did. He was the once and future King of England.

For one anniversary party, a very special party, I had done some heavy research and, wonder of wonders, had found a group of Viennese musicians who had played at a coffeehouse in Vienna that the Duke had frequented. One of the violinists even remembered the special song that the Duke had requested time after time in that small coffeehouse. I couldn't wait till the evening of the party.

After my guests had been seated for dinner, the musicians took their places, unseen, in a corner of the foyer that adjoined the dining room. They were instructed to be still during the first course and the entrée.

The Duke sat down to his favorite dish, rare roast beef thinly sliced, as thin as one could slice, with horseradish. If you're going to serve the ex–King of England roast beef, it's imperative to do it correctly. The Duke sat at one end of the table in a lavish red velvet chair and the Duchess sat opposite him in a similar chair. She wore a Windsor blue Yves St. Laurent dress, a diamond and sapphire choker, and a very proper air of constrained upper class.

Before dessert, the strains of the song the Duke loved best in the world wafted gently into the room. He stared in delight and his eyes grew large and round. "Where is that music coming from, Estée?" he breathed. "Who is that playing?"

"They're Viennese musicians, Your Highness," I said. "I brought them here to play for you."

He ate nothing further—just listened raptly. When we were finished, we rose to leave the room, and the musicians, now in sight, bowed deeply to the Duke. He was, to them, still King.

And the Duke became the King again. He acknowledged the bow, stood straighter, and led us to the drawing room for after-dinner drinks. We all watched him with happiness. His posture, his joy, were something to see.

The Duke stood, when he received his drink, and the room held its breath. He wanted to speak. It was a touching moment. "I didn't intend to make a speech," he said. "You know, I never have before at any other party you've given us, Estée," he said. "Still, I just want to tell you and your wonderful guests that the thirty years I've spent with my lovely Duchess have been the most wonderful of my life."

I watched his Duchess. She sat stiffly, as she usually did, but she was smiling so *youngly*. Clearly, she was as moved as we.

All night long the musicians played. The Duke, cane in hand, danced with a lightness of spirit. My daughter-in-law Evelyn is from Vienna. She is very charming and very natural. At one point, she began to hum a melody her mother sang to her when she was small, and the Duke knew it and sang right along. And they danced, the Duke and Evelyn, in the candlelight, caught by the mirrored walls. That evening, I saw the man and the King in the Duke.

The next morning, very early, the telephone rang. I was fast asleep and I reached over Joe to answer.

"Estée? Duke speaking," said the caller.

"Duke who?" I asked with a yawn. And then . . .

"Oh, forgive me, Your Highness. *The* Duke, of course."

"That was the sweetest night of my life," he said. "And I just wanted to thank you for it, with the music still ringing in my ears."

SWEET FRIENDS

I remember where we met. Having a business lunch at Maxim's one day with Françoise de la Renta, who was then executive editor of *Vogue*, I mentioned I was leaving for America the next morning on the SS *United*

States. I hate to fly—I've always preferred an ocean and a boat to an airplane.

"Oh," she said. "The Duke and Duchess are going on the same ship. You really should get to know her because she loves your cosmetics. "In fact," said Françoise, "she told me that Elizabeth Arden's man comes in to make her up before parties and he invariably uses Estée Lauder products."

That was encouraging news. I liked the Duchess already and I admired the taste of Elizabeth Arden's makeup man.

"I'll tell her you'll be aboard," said Françoise, who loved to make matches.

I was unabashedly thrilled that first night when a purser came to our suite and said that His Royal Highness, the Duke of Windsor, would be pleased if we joined him for cocktails before dinner in his suite.

He'd be pleased! I was quivering. I'd have taken a long route to this place. And now, the ex-King would be pleased if I'd come for drinks. Then nervousness set in. Fortunately, there wasn't much time to worry. I put on my best Dior—I had heard Dior was the Duchess's favorite designer. When we arrived at their cabin, we felt as though we'd known them always—they were so warm. I got my first taste of the Duchess's skill at entertaining that first night. She was quite seductive, with a very subtle appeal; I could see why the man gave up a kingdom for her. And she was so cheerful and gay.

We talked about cosmetics. And treatment products. "I can use all you have," she said graciously.

"Oh, no, your skin is lovely," I protested. The Duchess was obsessed by the desire to appear always as young as she looked when a king gave up his throne for her. That was not really possible, although she could come close. When her efforts compromised her health, her friends worried. I remember, years later, when she called me to ask me to plead with my good friend Dr. Baer in London to agree to give her yet another face lift. We were both upset when he said it would be medically imprudent to do so, but for different reasons. The Duchess was so lovely in her maturity, her skin was so supple, you'd think she'd have known it. Often, the people you'd think would be most confident in the world are the least sure of themselves.

On this first evening together, the Duchess stopped herself from asking me beauty questions (even though I strongly sensed she had a million more) and drew me over to another couple.

"It's time to speak with others," she said with a smile, "so you'll know everyone here." This was to be her "hostess" pattern, I noted, in the years that passed. And it worked, making her parties warm and appealing.

"Please, don't sit near the partner you had at dinner!" she'd call out as we left her dining table for after-dinner drinks. And, because of her insistence, we were all bolder and reached out to others. I always left her parties feeling as though I'd met so many interesting people, and that was the Duchess's intention.

Once, in Paris, at her summer home, the Duchess invited us to high tea, which resembled an afternoon luncheon. Her lovely silver was gleaming as though she expected her mother-in-law for lunch instead of just Joe and me. We had the *tiniest* sandwiches and scones and jam. The Duchess ordered tea and milk for herself and the Duke, and tea and lemon for Joe and me. (Afterward, I tried tea and milk and came to prefer it.) That day, I remember, we'd brought two copies of a photograph of the four of us that had been taken in my Palm Beach home. We knew the Duke was failing and I did so want a signed memento of our times together. The extra copy was brought as a gift for the two of them. The Duke took the photograph, walked over to a delicate desk piled high with books, and said, "On this desk, Joe, I signed my abdication papers. I haven't written on it since that day, but today I will, to sign this photo of friendship."

We were all silent and quite moved. To break the inevitable sadness of memory, the Duchess chimed in with, "What about me? I want to sign also!"

She took the copy meant for them and signed her name on it.

"Hang this one in your office, Estée," she said chuckling. "It will remind you to send me your newest antiaging product."

I might add that both Joe and the Duke had a royal constitution for holding down four or five Scotches without visible effect.

I think the Duke most appreciated Joe's unpretentious manner. They would exchange jokes, little stories; they adored each other. It almost seemed to me as though the Duke had no one else who treated him as a real person, and Joe knew no other way to treat anyone except as a real person. Which didn't stop Joe from making a little joke when Raymond Bermay, director of Estée Lauder in France, asked how he addressed the Duke of Windsor. "As little as possible," said Joe.

PARTY BLUEPRINT

We were talking about parties, weren't we? Let me tell you some things I've learned about the perfect evening.

INVITATIONS   If the party numbers fewer than ten, a handwritten invitation is called for. If one is planning a *very* large and formal party, a printed invitation is best.

FIRST THINGS FIRST   Be near the entrance when your guests arrive. How many times have you gone to a large party and looked for ten minutes for a sign of your hosts? That's poor taste. A great, welcoming smile sets the mood for the evening. Everyone appreciates a warm greeting.

Introduce people to each other by giving them "handles": a few words on who is who and who does what is thoughtful and starts conversation rolling.

THE DINING ROOM   Entering the room where you'll dine should be a sensual experience. Aromas must be gentle—no scorched filet ema-

Gloria Swanson was my biggest
Youth Dew fan. Leonard and Joe are
in the background.

Joan Crawford; this most gracious
hostess literally took the cloth from
her dining-room table and gave it to
me after I admired it.

Tiaras were "in" at the April in Paris Ball
in 1965, and Bette Davis and I made the
most of the style…

One of the sweetest swash-
bucklers of all time, Douglas
Fairbanks, Jr.

Lauren Bacall and I at a Parisian
fashion show.

Bob Hope (*left*) never goes anywhere without his Aramis—or so
it seems to me. Mrs. Hope
(*second from right*) approves.

Frank Sinatra with Nancy Reagan
campaigning in Westchester.

Walter Cronkite, the most trusted voice in television news.

My darling friend, the Begum Aga Khan, at our home for dinner.

C. Z. Guest and her daughter, Cornelia, at a luncheon several years ago. C. Z. is a celebrated beauty, and her daughter is now a lovely debutante.

Four women with three very different lives: *Left to right*: Virginia Masters, the author and sex therapist; Helen Gurley Brown, Editor of *Cosmopolitan* and Estée and Evelyn Lauder.

An elegant man, Givenchy, and couturier to the world of exquisite taste.

Ann Phillips

An embrace from the grand lady of fashion: Diana Vreeland.

A wonderful party *chez* Lauder. Princess
Grace of Monaco is sixth from the left,
flanked by Douglas Fairbanks, Jr., and Joe.

Mrs. John MacLean and
Mrs. Laddie Sanford at a costume party.

Place cards for a dinner honoring the
Duke and Duchess of Windsor were
reproductions of the Fabergé eggs
she so loved.

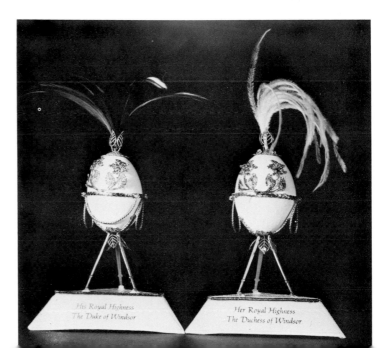

His Royal Highness
The Duke of Windsor

Her Royal Highness
The Duchess of Windsor

Having lovely portraits taken is part of every woman's fantasy. Realizing this fantasy was a thrill, but it served a purpose as well, for publicity is a very big part of my job.

Snowden as seen in *Vogue*

Mrs. Alva Gimbel, of Saks Fifth Avenue
and Gimbel Brothers Department stores,
at my George Washington's Birthday party.
Red, white and blue were the colors,
and I can't remember a more festive evening.

Mort Kaye

There is nothing more perfect, more gala,
more exciting than a White House dinner.
I'm at the left, listening to President
Ford, and Evelyn, in the white dress,
is behind me.

Left to Right: Mrs. Vincent
Astor and I with
Mrs. Albert Lasker
and Mr. August Hecksher
receiving an architectural
award for outstanding work in
beautifying New York City.

Mr. Cornelius Vanderbilt
Whitney and I, attending a
party in Palm Beach.

Bob Davidoff

nating from the kitchen, please. The gleam of the silver, the sheen of the wood, the flickering of the candles, should be breathtakingly beautiful. Flowers should be unique and different, not your standard bouquet of carnations or mums. The *balance* of the room should be harmonious and pleasing. Dishes should sparkle! Even if you've washed every one after your last week's party, wash them again. Silver should be polished until you can see your face in it clearly, then polished and polished again, then buffed with a soft cloth. Crystal must be absolutely clear. Perfection is the byword of a party. Does that sound fanatic? So be it. My guests feel wonderfully cheered, I think, and cherished and *important* in a room that I've lovingly prepared for them.

PERSONAL INVOLVEMENT   Just as I have a very clean finger in every pot of cream, lotion, and scent that comes with my name on it, I personally decide and supervise every aspect of a party.

You may think that it's easy for me to have perfect parties because expense is no object. You'd be wrong if you thought that. It's effort and time—not dollars—that make an occasion beautiful. On *any* budget I guarantee you that my parties would be just as perfect in detail. One exquisite flower in a simple container can be as magnificent as a roomful of flowers. Taste and scale should reign, no matter how much you have to spend.

In my early entertaining days, we'd have buffets and arrange everything ourselves in the morning. My husband would help with the drinks, and everyone would serve himself. Even if you can afford the best, you still have to know to *choose* the best butchers, the best cuts of meat, the freshest flowers and vegetables. You have to know that a leg of lamb can be boned. Therefore, I say, educate yourself if you wish to have fine parties to share with your friends and business associates. Read! There are many wonderful ''how to'' books on the market. I'm always browsing through bookstores for new ideas from innovative celebrators. Having an unlimited budget doesn't guarantee style, elegance, and originality. For that, you have to have imagination. And that costs nothing.

But, again—I will repeat it—perfection is the byword of a party. Every detail just so. The perfection, of course, must appear to be absolutely effortless, as if no trouble at all was involved.

Perhaps there's *nothing* quite as festive and perfect as a White House state dinner. You arrive at the famous gate with your name, perhaps a photograph, on an identifying piece of paper, a social security number— it differs each time—and then the information is matched against the guard's master list of invitees. If your car has a special sticker that you've been issued previously, you may be allowed to drive right up to the doors of the White House, but usually the cars are lined up so far back it's better to get out and walk once you've passed the initial guardpost, as Frank and Barbara Sinatra and I did the last time we all went to a state dinner. The music is playing as you arrive and your name is announced to join the receiving line and be greeted by the President and his wife. At dinner, the tables are set magnificently, and soon a hot consommé or a cold jellied soup is served, along with a four-course meal and an innovative dessert. Then there is music or dancing in another room. The level of conversation is always stimulating; on one side of you may sit an important business executive, on another a senator, and always there's the special aura that surrounds the President of the United States and his beautiful wife. I've been privileged to dine with the Reagans, the Carters, the Fords, the Nixons. I had a special fondness for the young and dashing President Kennedy, who often came to visit his mother, my friend and neighbor in Palm Beach.

LIGHTING   Party lighting sets the mood. Harsh, unflattering glare creates an oppressive atmosphere. Rosy, flattering-to-all candlelight casts a romantic festive air. I love *armloads* of candles in a dining room, not the obligatory one or two. At any given dinner party I may use a dozen or more candles, with the only other light coming, perhaps, from an illuminated painting.

At the table, candles should never have an overpowering fragrance to interfere with the aroma of the food, but a mildly scented candle, placed strategically here and there, is quite wonderful. It masks the odor of the furniture polish you used in the afternoon, the silver polish, or anything else that's been used in party preparation. Once I attended a party where masses of candles were clustered and flickering in each of four corners in the room—what a wonderful effect!

TABLE   The table should be the focal point of the room and it should be worthy of inspiring a sharp intake of breath as your guests enter. I often use a gold or silver lamé cloth *under* magnificent ecru lace cloths; this has a festive, rich look but not a *shining* look because the lace mutes the gold and silver. When I use gold, I use vermeil accessories— vermeil salt cellars and pepper mills, dessert plates, salad forks. With the silver cloth, I use silver accessories, highlighted with my mother's twenty-fifth-anniversary silver service plates, with everything else silver as well. Incidentally, nothing looks as beautiful as silver reflected on mahogany, so I'll often do without a cloth altogether and use delicate linen placemats instead. Flowers on a table are lovely, of course, if they're not centerpieces, which are usually too high and block views. I happen to favor masses of lilies of the valley (the Duchess's favorite flowers) placed in six small antique silver tankards that range across the table. Don't restrict yourself to traditional flower containers for your table—any beautiful holder will do; the tankards were originally drinking cups, of course. During holiday time, I never use flowers; instead, I often use fruits or vegetables of the season. One holiday when I used a gold cloth under the lace one, I filled crystal compotes with golden kumquats, and my table looked divine. A huge silver bowl of the roundest, reddest apples can be lovely. Think about containers for flowers or fruits by casting an appraising eye around your house; there's no law that says a vase must be used. If you take a delicate candy dish, fill it with black rocks and one or two baby orchids, you have a Japaneses sculpture for your dinner table. Frogs are those tiny, green, many-spiked holders that can be placed in containers and hidden by ferns, and flowers spiked on them look professionally arranged.

A SPECIAL KIND OF TRIBUTE   Let me share a very effective *modus operandi* for parties. It's always so appreciated to give a party *in honor* of someone. It can be your best friend's birthday or a visit from an ambassador. Whatever the reason, it's the same party, the same amount of work, the same expense, with one extra splendid difference: you've given the limelight to someone you care about, someone who deserves a limelight, and everyone loves a limelight, every now and then! Your invitations, of course, specify this guest of honor's place at your hearth.

THE MENU   Menus placed at every third or fourth place add a very elegant touch and are a grand idea generally. I either handwrite or have printed on parchment paper or cream-colored menu cards the meal I've planned to serve. There isn't a guest who wouldn't prefer to know what will be served before beginning to eat. Should he concentrate on the first course because he really doesn't love the entrée? Should she save some calories for the soufflé or eat as much as she wants because the dessert is a simple, unfattening fruit?

WHAT DID YOU SAY YOUR NAME WAS?   At each person's place, I usually put a very pretty place card, shaped like a tent and mono-grammed with my initials. My daughter-in-law Evelyn has given me the good idea of hand-lettering my guest's name on *both* sides of the tent so the person sitting opposite will have a name for the face directly across. When placing guests, I try to think of my guests' personalities and with whom they might enjoy a chat. One can serve the finest food in the most elegant manner, but if a guest is seated next to a person he finds a deadly bore, the dinner party for that guest is ruined. One rule of thumb is that older men enjoy sitting near younger women and older women near younger men. An older woman near an older man ranks as the worst possible combination.

A general note about the people you invite: I've noticed that there are always those who are not generous of spirit at a party, who come with an attitude of "entertain me if you can!" These are clearly not your best guests. They will only watch, criticize, and talk unpleasantly afterward. Parties are for people who want to share themselves and who want to experience the best others have to offer. Fill your guest list with such friends. As a matter of fact, fill your *life* with such friends. Judgmental and carping people are no fun anywhere.

THE TABLE SURPRISE   Surprises make a party. For special occasions, I make sure there is a memento at each place setting for each person to take home. This gesture never fails to be appreciated, even by ultra-sophisticates, who consider themselves too wordly-wise for mementos. They're the first to smile broadly with delight as they open their gifts!

I often select a small object and have it monogrammed, so each gift is individual and personal. Another option for me has always been my products; they're never met with anything but delight. Who wouldn't love a small, gleaming compact filled with solid perfume or a stunning bottle of men's cologne—at Easter time, a luscious chocolate egg; at Christmas, a gift for each under the tree.

In addition to the regular menu, I often have the menu printed on a fine linen handkerchief as another memento.

Table surprises always seem to be so appreciated that I provide them at home parties *and* at promotional parties.

THE MUSICAL SURPRISE   Music plays a fine part in enlivening the mood of a party. One year, a week before Christmas, Princess Grace, Her Serene Highness, was coming to dinner. What to do? I racked my brain and finally had it. I asked a Salvation Army group, complete with five singers, uniforms, tambourines—everything—to stand just inside the entrance way as Grace arrived. When she saw the huge Christmas tree, the holly, and the mistletoe, and heard the Salvation Army band singing the traditional carols that they sing better than anyone else in the world, her eyes filled with tears.

"This is *so* . . . *Christmas*," she said. "It makes me homesick and terribly happy at the same time."

Christmas trees don't have to be green, by the way. I've had them white and blue, red and white and silver. One year, when the Austrian ambassador to the United Nations was visiting, we hung our tree with antique Viennese music boxes.

Wonderful music has such a broad range. A barbershop quartet dressed in straw boaters and bow ties, a trio of folk singers, one violinist or a group of Elizabethan-costumed students from the Juilliard School singing madrigals, all contribute to the mood of a party.

Sometimes, if the occasion calls for it, music should be formal. I once gave a party in honor of Florence Gould in the antique English section of New York's Metropolitan Museum of Art. Mrs. Gould had just presented the museum with an enormous Bonnard painting. I'd researched the era and even had the tables set with some of the museum's own English silver, with the curator's permission, naturally. Everything was gray-blue-white elegant; white-gloved waiters served, and twenty-two tuxedoed violinists played on the balcony. It was quite an *effect*! After dinner, the guests had coffee in the huge room where Mrs. Gould's Bonnard was hung. One guest asked Mrs. Gould, "When you took down your big Bonnard and gave it to the museum, what did you ever find to put in its place?"

Florence Gould, whose husband was the youngest son of Jay Gould, one of the country's most famous millionaires, answered quite simply, "I just hung another one there."

What else?

Another time, I gave a party in honor of the Spanish ambassador to the United Nations. After the meal, the guests were ushered into a large Tudor-style drawing room, where a fire blazed cozily and butlers served cognac.

Suddenly a gentleman in a dinner jacket, someone everyone else assumed was a guest, began to sing softly from one corner of the room. The guests looked up, startled and delighted. From the opposite corner, a woman in a beautiful ballgown began to answer him in song. From each corner of the room, four singers I'd hired from the New York City Opera sang medleys of old Broadway tunes and light opera in such a rousing, beautiful, Nelson Eddy–Jeanette MacDonald fashion that the room *rang* with my guests' applause after each number. It was an unforgettable evening!

Music is really the quintessential "puller-together." Generally, it must not be obtrusive and it must not last too long, but if done with style, show me the guest who doesn't love it!

PARTY THEMES   *Themes are fun* for a party. In every one of us lies a need to make believe. Once you get over the initial shyness, there's nothing more festive than a costume party that allows men and women to imagine themselves someone else, somewhere else. Joe, I must admit, never *quite* conquered his reluctance to dress up in a costume, although he was a splendid sport and played along for my sake. The closest he came to rebellion was when we were once advised to "wear something gold" to a party. He refused to dress according to the instruction, but he assured me that all would be fine when we arrived at the party. When Hebe Dorsey, the fabulous editor of the international *Herald Tribune*, asked, "Joe, where's your gold touch?" he opened his mouth to display a gold tooth. Joe is also the man who once bragged that he was the only person in America ever to wear out a tuxedo.

Despite his total lack of enthusiasm for costume parties, I always looked forward to dressing up. One of the most memorable dressing-ups took place at a party I gave in honor of George Washington's birthday. I had an airline fly down a planeload of cherries, with which my garden trees were festooned. The Brooke Costume House outfitted the waiters in breeches and satins à la George, and we all wore period costumes.

Wearing a fun disguise is, if nothing else, probably the world's most effective and *immediate* ice breaker. Nothing opens a conversation faster than coming face to face with a knight in shining armor. *If you're a good sport, that is.*

Good conversation is, of course, the flavor of every party. Despite rumor, I've found that people who genuinely love parties are exciting and excitable and need few props for conversation. For those who have difficulty opening up to strangers, a warm and generous comment will usually work.

And then, at some parties, one may always encounter the bore. Pity the sad bore! My experience has told me he often knows he's boring but can't do anything about it. If you dig deep enough, there is always something interesting to be found in everyone, always a new insight or idea to be gathered if you ask the right questions. Still, sometimes you just want to escape. That's reasonable also. I'm often amused by the tactics some use.

Traditionally, diplomats carry two drinks with them during the cocktail hour, which allows them, when cornered by a bore, to bow and say, "Will you excuse me, please, I have to deliver this drink." Another popular ploy is to wave at some invisible person at the other end of the room and say to the bore, "Do please excuse me. Francine [or whoever] wants me to meet her friend from out of town."

WHAT LIES BEHIND THE TRUFFLES?

Plenty. Mostly, planning, planning, planning. In your mind, "walk" your whole party through from beginning to end and figure out *times*—

cooking times, serving times, conversation times. Regarding conversation: I never let the cocktail hour last an hour. Forty-five minutes is just enough. Guests tend to wax maudlin after that amount of time. Cocktails, moreover, are never served with complicated, heavy hors d'oeuvres to laden digestion and sabotage the enjoyment of the meal to follow. The working word is "light" when it comes to snacks with drinks. My daughter-in-law Jo Carole has noted that many guests don't like the heaviness of bread, so she serves pâté or special cheeses on delicate endive leaves. What a wonderful hors d'oeuvre! I've adapted it to serve fine rosettes of caviar mixed with a bit of sour cream or paper-thin slices of smoked salmon garnished with capers.

The very best tip for party food I can offer is this: prepare your own first course and your own dessert and make them simply extraordinary. This is the true, deep-down secret of a successful dinner; people tend to remember what they ate first and what they ate last and rarely what came in between. You can have the in-between courses catered, but do your guests the honor of preparing the first and last courses yourself. It doesn't have to be a strain, even for a very busy woman.

FIRST COURSE   It's very often a fabulous soup. I love soups. My favorites are a cold jellied borscht served in individual soup plates with a dollop of sour cream and a teaspoon of fresh caviar served on top. Or, a not-too-thick and not-too-thin vegetable soup cooked the day before and served with some delicate crackers.

Another favorite first course is broiled fresh crabmeat in a cream sauce, served brown and bubbling in individual shells. A variation of this is crabmeat served in the center of a rice mold with Russian dressing and dill.

MAIN COURSE   Are you rushed for time? There is nothing quicker and more impressive (no preparation on your part) than a crown roast of lamb. The butcher prepares these baby rib chops in an upright position with ground lamb used as a stuffing in the center. It's a festive and visually appealing dish, especially when served with tiny paper frills on each bone end. All you have to do is roast and serve to general acclaim.

For a fish entrée I often poach a whole salmon and serve it garnished with paper-thin slices of cucumber and lemon. Accompanied by a light, fresh dill sauce, this is presentation in its finest form. Serving even the plainest food with presentation makes it taste splendid, adds elegance to the meal!

If I decide to serve fowl, I like a boned and stuffed individual squab, baked and served with a side dressing of guava jelly. Champagne added during the cooking gives it a delicious zest, and the bird, served in a ring of wild rice with hearts of artichokes and tiny fresh mushrooms on the side, is wonderful.

After the main course, I serve a salad to cleanse the palate. A delightful one is endive, watercress, and white seedless grapes.

DESSERT   I love a rhubarb and strawberry pie served warm. My pear dessert is very simple and chic. This consists of peeled pears with stems intact cooked in red wine to which a little water and sugar have been added. I simmer the pears slowly for about two hours, or until they are soft but definitely still quite whole; I leave the pears to soak in the wine overnight at room temperature (not in the refrigerator). When dessert time is nigh, I soften some good vanilla ice cream and spoon it into a crystal bowl, stand the pears around the edge of the bowl, stem up, grate some slivers of bittersweet chocolate over the ice cream, and serve with small cookies. Or, if I'm in a hurry, I leave a can of drained crushed pineapple mixed with a few tablespoons of crème de menthe to soak overnight in the refrigerator. For dessert, I place softened vanilla ice cream in a crystal bowl, cover it with the crème de menthe pineapple, grate some fresh ginger over the mixture, and serve with cookies or petits fours.

COFFEE   I like to serve Irish coffee occasionally—the men seem to love it. More often I serve a demitasse with a sliver of lemon peel.

After dinner, I do something quite old-fashioned and very popular in England. If I have a large group of people, the men are guided into one room and the women into another for after-dinner drinks. You may of course skip this tradition, but I find it makes for an interesting change of conversation and atmosphere for a very short while. I don't mean to say that only the men will discuss big business—quite the contrary! In my world, the women guests are just as often the high-powered achievers as the men. Still, there's something nice and old-fashioned about the tradition. It lends piquancy to the evening.

PARTIES AND EXPECTATION

My social life and my business life seem to flow from the same source: the desire to be good, close to perfect, at what I do. When I entertain, my expectations are high and my standards even higher—just as they are when I'm mixing a new fragrance. There is no contradiction between giving parties and mixing creams: both have to be extraordinary to be acceptable.

One of the most festive parties I ever attended was not one I gave at all. It was held in Venice and it was really a ball, not a party, designed to raise money for the city during the time of the Venice floods. Princess Irene Galitzine, the wonderful couturière, was on the committee that issued the invitations, and she made me a gown and mask that were perfectly lovely. Earl Blackwell, of *Celebrity Register* fame and a dear friend, had organized the affair. Since he was using Charles Revson's yacht *Ultima II* as a base in Venice, Revson also received an invitation. Earl knew Revson wouldn't be happy if I was present. Revson was never happy if I was within ten miles of him, and yet I encountered him almost everywhere I went. Though he hated parties, I believe he felt he had to be seen where and when I was seen. An active social life was abhorrent to him but he forced himself to be prominent in the public eye so I'd not have an advantage.

He thought I wouldn't be coming to the Venice ball. He was so happy about that! When he saw the photographers thronging around me and Her Serene Highness, Princess Grace, Mr. Revson's face became rigid and white with anger. Strange man.

THE PERFECT GUEST

Before I ever entertain, I feel I owe it to my guests to lie down for a short, half-hour rest before I dress. It refreshes me and restores my energy. Before I go to a party, I do the same thing, so I can be the best guest in the world.

Being the best guest also means expressing appreciation after a party. I usually telephone or send a note with some nice words about how I enjoyed the evening. For a special occasion, I might send a small gift. If I decide to send flowers, I have them delivered the *morning* of the party, not in the evening, when the hostess is greeting the guests and won't appreciate having to scurry around for a proper container, and not the day after, when the house is still filled with the hostess's choice of flowers.

Once, as a *guest*, I received a gift—after I left a luncheon party at Joan Crawford's home. It was the perfect gesture of gift giving and I've never forgotten the gracious impulse that inspired it. I had admired a hand-embroidered tablecloth at Joan's table. After we ate, we went into the living room for coffee. The butler entered with a wrapped package and said, "This came for Mrs. Lauder a few minutes ago."

"A package came for me? *Here?*" I asked with some surprise. Well, it could have been an urgent shipment of fragrances which my office could have sent by messenger.

"Open it when you get home, please, dear," said Joan. "I have no scissors down here." Of course, when I arrived home and opened the package, it was the lovely cloth I had admired. The note read, "Please accept this, my dear friend. I never know what to give you for your kindnesses and I was so happy you liked this tablecloth!"

Let spontaneity be your guide as to an expression of thanks to your hosts—or to your guests, as Joan demonstrated.

THE GOOD LIFE

"The good life" means different things to different people, of course. I know many wonderful people who feel complete with hearth, home, and companions in one place, who feel satisfied with a small but loving circle of friends and family.

I relish reaching out to the world and its infinite beauty! I love the look and sound of people from both faraway places and near. I feel best fulfilled when I am sampling the best of different climes, foods, atmospheres, and people.

My life is comfortable, but I know that my joy in sunshine, friends, and color would bring me the same great happiness if I didn't have much more than a penny. There is so much to do . . . and so much to enjoy. One must seize the moment, always.

I must admit one thing though. It is such satisfaction to know that my own great efforts, my intuition and risk taking, have brought me the means to enjoy the kind of good life I love.

CHAPTER 12

THE MOST BEAUTIFUL FACE IN THE WORLD

The most beautiful face in the world? It's not Elizabeth Taylor's, not Christie Brinkley's, not Brooke Shields's—it's yours. This is not advertising copy—it's what I truly believe. The reason why *your* face is so beautiful is that it's unique. It has your incredible depth and personality written all over it. It has your creativity and radiance.

Perfect features won't do it. I know many women with soft, huge eyes, rosebud mouths, and Katharine Hepburn cheekbones, and you still wouldn't turn around to look at them in the street. You know these women also. They're, well, sweet-looking, but missing something. What they're missing is glow. Mother Nature doesn't have a premium on beauty. If she did, natural rosebud mouths would have a plummier, deeper color, eyelashes would be fringier, and everyone would be born with a natural glow. But everyone isn't born with a glow. Therefore, makeup was invented.

Chanel once said, "Wear makeup; it's so conceited not to!" I know just what she meant. It inevitably turns out that women who reject makeup are either those who feel hopeless about their chances of improving themselves or those whose vanity tells them they're perfect. Both groups are wrong. Skin care and makeup can make *anyone* look wonderful, and I've never met anyone who couldn't benefit from knowing the marvelous ways of creams and cosmetics. The lure of makeup is irresistible because it promises not just dreams but reality. There isn't a man or woman alive who isn't interested in being attractive to others. The busier they are and the more dynamic and exciting they are, the more interested in looking attractive they are.

Men do not look at dresses; they look at faces. Women do not look at ties or suits; they look at faces. The first impression is the one that counts most strongly.

"But I like the natural look," you murmur. You'll still have to use makeup. I, too, like the natural look, but I know that the natural beauties of our time all use soft makeup, artfully applied. No woman beyond her early teens should go around with a naked or half-dressed face and expect to make a great impression on anyone. In fact, women need cosmetics and skin care more than ever because glamour, in an active woman's life, is not so much an indulgence anymore as a necessity. Whether you *are* the chairperson of the board or you want to charm him, you need beauty and femininity as well as wisdom and strength. If you're a man, you need to look vigorous and in control, and you need to smell clean. Women have been rightfully encouraged to express feelings of selfhood—express and satisfy them. Deciding to take control of the way you look is a strong way of doing just that. It's easy to look careless, colorless, and sloppy. All you have to do is let yourself go.

Take an old suit and an old face, wear them to work and you look drab, old. But take the same old suit, freshen it up with a scarf and some pretty makeup, wear it to work, and you're high style. Fashions in faces, I am fond of saying, move much faster than fashions in clothes. Cleopatra eyes, a ghostly pallid mouth, and a beauty mark will date you more quickly than a ten-year-old dress.

"But I have no time for all that," you might reply.

It *takes* barely any time at all to be beautiful. When a woman has her cosmetics handy and has spent some time in practice sessions, three or four minutes to make up her face is absolutely all that's needed! Any longer and you're doing something wrong. I know the current fad is for complicated facials and hour-long makeups, but to that I say nonsense. With all that's available in the marketplace, you should be able to have a glowing skin and a radiant, fresh look in easy minutes, not tedious hours.

Most women, I've discovered, don't worry all that much about chronological aging. We're resigned to it, and science has managed to prolong our years to almost twice what our grandparents expected. What we do worry about is the *look* of aging. All around us are associates who look very young—*much* younger than we *ever* were.

The bad news is that we will grow older. The good news is that we *can* control the signs of aging. Time is not on your side, but I am. And it's not just aging we should be concerned with. It's making the absolute most of what we have. I must repeat one of my favorite maxims—there are no homely women, only careless ones. Beauty is glow and fragrance. Beauty is the will to be beautiful. You have to want it very much and then help it along with some well-chosen products. Nothing gives you a lift more than "playing" with new colors on you face. If you use a new lipstick, a new blusher, a mascara that makes *fringes* out of your lashes, glow that makes you softly radiant, you feel better when you look in the mirror. Your lover's face lights when he sees you. Your children want to touch you—the beautiful-mommy syndrome is a strong and memorable one (the beautiful-smelling-mommy syndrome rates up there also). Somehow, the work is easier when you feel and look lovely. The smiles greeting you are more genuine.

What's more discordant than a woman dressed in the latest style, yet with skin as dry as a bone? Her shoes are expensive, but her makeup's last year's look. Her portfolio is substantial, but her hair is teased and stiff. When I see her, even in an elevator or in a department store, I am still tempted to reach out and pat a little moisturizer on her skin.

A woman's skin should have a cared-for look.

THE ROUTINE

The first and most important thing you can do for yourself is to establish a skin-beauty routine. Please don't plan on elaborate rituals. You'll never stick to them. Just three minutes every morning and evening is all it should *ever* take.

If there's one word that sums up the revolutionary thinking of today's woman (and her man, as well, lately), it's care. It's the foundation without which no cosmetics will work. Sophisticated skin care can definitely give you a more supple, silken skin, and that means care that can fit into the corner of a briefcase, let alone a corner of your medicine cabinet. Skin care depends on your individual type of skin. See an expert behind any of our counters to determine *your* type.

THE LESS-THAN-THREE-MINUTES NIGHT-CARE PROGRAM

Every night, cleanse your skin. Never ever miss a night, no matter how tired you are. Use either a very pure and gentle soap and water (depending on your kind of skin) or an excellent lubricating cleanser. If you use the cleanser, pat it on, then tissue if off immediately. Apply some Night Repair, which helps speed the natural repair of damaged cells and binds moisture to the skin. Follow with your nourishing lubricating cream: work in a few drops until they are absorbed and take off the excess (don't waste it—rub it into your hands!). If your skin is very oily, use only the Night Repair and a drop of eye cream, which everyone can benefit from. Remember, even if you have a predominantly oily skin, you can still *spot-moisturize* the few dry spots instead of applying lubricating cream over the entire area. Spots to check for dryness are the laugh lines on the side of the mouth, as well as the tiny lines around the outside of the eyes. A drop of cream on the throat never hurts either. *Fini!*

ESTÉE LAUDER'S LESS-THAN-THREE-MINUTES MAKEUP

IN THE MORNING   Are you seeing someone off—a husband, lover, or child? Apply just a touch of blusher on your face to say goodbye: let those closest to you have a lovely image of the woman they just left. Then, apply the following makeup, from the products that are all ready and waiting:

First: Three of four drops of moisturizer on the skin. Work in well; don't blot. Re-Nutriv or Swiss Performing Extract are perfect.

Second: A little glow comes next. As you smile, put the color higher toward the cheekbones (a coral or a rose blusher is beautiful). The glow, applied *under* the foundation, makes the radiance seem to come from within!

Third: Now apply your foundation base (preferably one with a sun block built in: Polished Performance is such a base). Work in a few drops until you have a smooth, natural, and lovely-looking color all over!

Fourth: Give yourself that *finished* look with a cream-based powder lightly patted over the entire face.

Fifth: Apply a bit more powder blusher (the glow) over the powder to deepen the radiance.

Sixth: Eye shadow comes next. I like two shades, a darker one on the lid and a lighter one blended into the darker and rising toward the brow. There shouldn't be a line of demarcation where one shadow begins and another ends. Blend, blend!

Seventh: The eyeliner should meld with the lash line and be gently smudged so it doesn't look hard.

Eighth: Mascara can be applied in coats and you can powder your lashes in between the coats to create greater staying power.

Ninth: Lipstick is last. Apply it neither over or under your natural lip line but *follow* the natural line. A bit of gloss applied in the center of the bottom lip makes luscious lips.

And that's it. How long did it take? More than three minutes? Speed up your application. Applying makeup should (and eventually will, with practice) be like brushing your teeth—a natural, instinctive, and speedy act.

Remember, if you're a blonde, you need a bit more makeup in the evening hours than your brunette sister.

I remember being at a wonderful party with the great beauty, C. Z. Guest. She didn't look quite so beautiful as she had when we met just that afternoon as a matter of fact. I knew why—and told her.

"Blondes fade out at night, C.Z.," was my advice. "You need a little glow."

She's still repeating that line. Recently she had to introduce me at a luncheon and she did so as "the woman who informed me that blondes fade out at night . . ."

ADVICE FROM MY HEART

Everywhere I go, I reach out and touch—and then I answer questions. I seem to hear the same questions over and over from women who want simple answers but seem to receive only complicated theories. I offer here some basic advice, tips that apply to everyone no matter what her skin type or coloring. There is nothing mysterious or difficult about giving yourself the most beautiful face in the world. All it requires is common sense, knowledge of what's available, and practice, practice, practice. When you were a little girl, didn't you love best to play with your mother's makeup? Well, play with your own colors, experiment, and find what works in the most natural way for your face.

The most important thing to remember, in my opinion, is that one must be *finished* in her look. Presenting a unified, completed look upon entrance into a room is the only way to feel secure in your looks. Prepare before your entrance. Don't finish on the way by pulling at your hair or dress or wiping the oil off your nose.

One way to be sure you are finished is to check your daytime makeup in the daylight. Keep a mirror by the window so you can see what everyone else will see.

Avoid extremes. Don't try for effects that make you stand out in the crowd. This is unattractive and tasteless. The orange and purple hair crowd won't agree, I'm certain.

Is it sexist to say that women do want to look beautiful for men? They do, you know. They also want to look beautiful for other women and for themselves. Be aware of your infinite possibilities. You are a potential beauty.

Here are some basic tips. Please consider them carefully, choose what applies to you, and act on those. What awaits you is confidence in your appearance.

• What are lips, after all, but to kiss? Look closely at yours. They aren't just one shade of color, are they? They're many shades. For that reason, I love two shades of lipstick on a mouth instead of just one. Two add more texture and depth than one shade. Try a tender mouth, for instance, with coral as the underlying shade and soft red or pink over it. The one color lips should never be is brown; nothing is more aging. Bright reds, soft pinks, gentle peaches, are best.

• *Your makeup should never precede you but walk with you.* No one loves seeing a flash of blue eyes, a glint of red lips, before the whole woman appears. Another word for this is softness.

• A rainy, gloomy day is no day to forget your makeup. You should make up especially carefully on gray days to bring the sunshine back! Fragrance on such days is an absolute spirit lifter.

• The six-feet test is a good way to check to see if you're finished. Stand six feet away from your mirror, then walk toward it. Is any one thing preceding your entrance? Are lips, eyes, cheeks, dress *jumping out* at you? Be objective. If the answer is yes, you're not finished. A good makeup is having everything on your face, but looking as if you were born that way.

• Never "just run out for a few minutes" without looking your best. This is not vanity—it's self-liking. Your face is always on display. Why should you look like a faded Polaroid snapshot? Who's going to remember you that way? Never allow your husband or lover to leave in the morning without a visual image of you as beautiful. Believe me, he'll encounter many women in the course of the day who'll be wearing makeup and fragrance—maybe even (unlucky for you) my makeup and fragrance! Have *your* face be lovely in his memory.

• Never shine. I don't mind sheen, but I hate shine. It's oily-looking.

• Buy foundation in a shade that's slightly *lighter* than your natural skin color. A darker shade will only stain imperfections and make them more visible.

• Sunning is a national epidemic. I can't think of a single thing that is worse for your skin. It actually makes you seem eons older after a while, and it can be cancer-producing, as almost every responsible dermatologist warns. If you must expose your skin to the sun, be sure you buy the very best sun-protection creams that will allow you to tan while you screen out dangerous rays. Use moisturizers before and after sun exposure and reapply your sun cream every time before and after you go swimming. A woman of fifty who just loves the Florida sun is all cracked. I refer to her skin!

• Glow makes you look alive when everyone else looks pale and tired.

• Use a daytime makeup for the daylight hours and an evening makeup for the night hours. The daylight can make an evening makeup seem garish, and the yellow night lights can wash out a makeup meant for sunlight.

• Pink-Silk powder (we make it!) can make you look as glowing at night as you would after a vigorous tennis game.

• Color is important at the edge of the mouth. Don't let your lipstick fade out. Have you ever noticed how, as women age, their mouths begin to wear out? Make yours young and defined.

- Change makeup colors with the seasons. The paler colors you might wear with a suntan don't go well with fall fashion colors of brick and earth tones.

- Eye shadow should never be lighter than the actual eye; gimmicks and frostiness are for fifteen-year-olds. Remember, a sheen simply draws attention to imperfections. If you have tiny wrinkles, tiny creases on your lids, frosted anything will point an arrow to the very place you want to play down!

- Decide what you're wearing before you apply makeup to avoid clashing colors.

- Keep up with what's new in beauty. Dull, dated lipstick colors, flour-barrel face powder, and thick foundation make you look like last year's version.

- After you've finished your makeup, spray your hair with scent. It's mesmerizing for men when you dance.

- False eyelashes age you by ten years.

- A little blusher brushed onto the places where you naturally blush (chin and forehead, as well as cheeks) looks wonderful.

- If you fly in an airplane, drink, drink, drink. Water, not wine, please. Alcohol is a vasodilator, so one drink at 30,000 feet is like three. The best rule is to drink a glass of water for every hour of flying because the skin aspirates so much moisture. By the way, if you think you don't need to care for your skin meticulously, take out a mirror when you're at a 30,000-foot altitude and see what your skin really looks like when the light penetrates it more vividly than at any other time. You can even see blemishes and freckles that are *about* to come out! A chastening experience.

- Makeup can also be corrective. A second and far more perfect skin can cover scars, under-eye circles, broken capillaries, birth marks, blemishes, stretch marks, varicose veins—you name it. Opaque bases form camouflaging and protective coverings. If you can't get rid of the "thing" you hate on your face or body, you do have the power to make it disappear, at least for a little while.

• If you have broken blood vessels, blemishes, prominent veins or anything else you wish to hide or mute, gently tap some concealing cream on the area and blend it in. Concealer can make tired-looking under-eye puffs less visible; just apply some cream in dots on the line of demarcation *under* the puff and blend it gently with your fingertips. Don't put concealer directly *on* the puff; that will only call attention to it.

NO EXCUSE ACCEPTED

There's no excuse *not* to use makeup when it's so easily bought and applied. Recently a young woman in my office gave me a gift of a tiny makeup kit she'd found in an antique store. I could just see some old-style Theda Bara applying the colors to her face. But the kit was so unwieldy and the colors so artificial, no wonder Theda Bara had a chalk face! A tiny Sterno lamp to light the lash blackener came with the kit, and also a barley paste powder to be used for foundation, then a tiny pan of oily red color into which you'd dip your finger and transfer the "lipstick" to your mouth. That was makeup then! Think what a lark it is to buy and apply it today.

The miracle of makeup! Wherever I go, my message is always the same. Be all you can be. Be curious and experimental with what's available. Never forget that you don't lose your potential for beauty as you age. Experience and years may bring more lines, but they also bring more vitality and depth to a face. Pride in one's appearance is as important as pride in one's intelligence.

WISHES, DREAMS, AND VICTORIES

Frist comes the shy wish. Then you must have the heart to have the dream. Then, you work. And work.

From where you sit, you can probably reach out with comparative ease and touch a life of serenity and peace. You can wait for things to happen and not get too sad when they don't. That's fine for some but not for me. Serenity is pleasant, but it lacks the ecstasy of achievement.

I've insisted on the long stretch rather than the gentle reach. I celebrate this sweet country, where the work ethic and the beauty ethic walk hand in hand. America the Beautiful has given me a life of infinite value and pleasure.

In the jars and containers and tubes I sell are tiny slices of beauty—dreams come true. Beauty is not elusive after all. It's a reality made possible by wonderful creams and colors and an attitude of "Just look at me—I'm sparkling!"

Living the American dream has been intense, difficult work, but I couldn't have hoped for a more satisfying life. I believe that potential is unlimited—success depends on daring to act on dreams. How far do you want to go? Go the distance! Within each person is the potential to build the empire of her wishes, and don't allow anyone to say you can't have it all. You can—you *can* have it all if you're willing to work.

Which gave me more pleasure—the birth of a baby or the birth of a perfect fragrance that would bring joy to millions? Who can say? I chose not to choose between the two. No one has to settle for the mediocre if she has dreams of glory.

I've always believed that if you stick to a thought and carefully avoid distraction along the way, you can fulfill a dream. My whole life has been about fulfilling dreams. I kept my eye on the target, whatever that target was. I've never allowed my eye to leave the particular target of the moment, whether it was a lovely warm meeting with my adorable grandchildren, a business achievement, plans for an extraordinary party, or even just a quiet evening at home. Whether your target is big or small, grand or simple, ambitious or personal, I've always believed that success comes from not letting your eyes stray from that target. Anyone who wants to achieve a dream must stay strong, focused and steady. She must expect and demand perfection and never settle for mediocrity.

If you push yourself beyond the furthest place you think you can go, you'll be able to achieve your heart's dream.

When my darling Joe died in 1982, much of the light went out of my life. He was my best friend, the wing on which I flew, my confidant, lover, and partner. For a long time, nothing counted. The air I breathed was thin.

And then came murmurings of dissatisfaction with the new fragrance Estée Lauder was about to launch. It wasn't quite right. It was lovely, but it wasn't perfect. The family refused to go forward.

The challenge was irresistible. I jumped back into life. Somewhere Joe was smiling.

My sons, Leonard and Ronald, had a dream. They wanted to build a school at the University of Pennsylvania which would teach graduate students about business methods in various countries. If business people are sensitive to the differing ways of others, their goals are achieved far more easily. Just months before my sons announced our plans to donate such a school, Joe died. Leonard's son Gary and my daughter-in-law Jo Carole suggested we name it the Joseph H. Lauder Institute, and so we did. He would have been so proud.

I expect to be around for ages yet, playing NOSE, saying NO to anything less than perfection, and creating new fashions in faces and fragrances every step of my way. My company is *alive* with a dauntless spirit of its own, and my children and grandchildren are here to cheer it on and shepherd the pursuit of beauty to new wonders. I've passed them the baton of my conviction.

And if there is some heaven beyond earth, I'm sure it will be in the form of little angel girls, on high, who could use just the teeniest dab of blusher, just the *littlest* drop of Super-Rich All Purpose Creme, to make them look truly angelic. I'll be there, don't worry, to do the dabbing!

ABOUT THE AUTHOR

Estée Lauder is internationally famous as a great perfumer, an authority on scientific skin care, and designer of some of the most beautiful makeup colors in the world.

In addition to founding one of the most successful and prestigious businesses, she has lived an enormously fulfilling life as wife, mother, mother-in-law and grandmother. She is renowned as a hostess par excellence, and her inventive way of life is internationally admired.

Estée Lauder has received numerous awards and honors in recognition of her achievements in many fields. Those of which she is most proud include:

• *The Insignia of Chevalier of the Legion of Honor* awarded in 1978 by the government of France. Created by Napoleon in 1802, this is the highest award given by the French Republic for outstanding service in France. In presenting it, Consul General Gérard Gaussen said, "Mrs. Lauder represents what we French admire most about Americans—brains and heart."

• *The Gold Medal of the City of Paris*, awarded in 1979. This *Medaille de Vermeil* is the highest honor the city can bestow on a private citizen, and Ambassador Couve de Murville, former Prime Minister of France, said that it was, "not for any single accomplishment, but simply what she stands for, what she is, her singular genius."

• *The Crystal Apple from the Association for a Better New York*, presented in 1977 for "outstanding contribution to the city of New York." Examples of Mrs. Lauder's notable philanthropic work are the three world-famous adventure playgrounds for the children of New York City, created through the Estée and Joseph H. Lauder Foundation. This prompted the American Institute of Architects to present her with the *New York Women's Architectural Award of Honor* for "enhancement of the urban scene".

• *Recognition in 1970, by 575 business and financial editors, as one of the "Top Ten Outstanding Women in Business,"* the only woman in the cosmetic field to be cited.

• *Harper Bazaar's nomination as one of the 100 American Women of Accomplishment*, in 1967, and she has received many similar accolades since.

- *The Spirit of Achievement Award* received in 1968 from the Albert Einstein College of Medicine for "her unique skills and imagination . . . and for her lasting gifts of beauty that have delighted women everywhere . . ."

More recently, Cardinal Cooke has honored Mrs. Lauder in recognition of her philanthropic endeavors. Many charitable organizations, including National Cancer Care and the Manhattan League recognize her invaluable support and have paid her tribute.

In 1984 she was named—with Mrs. Barbara Bush, wife of George Bush, Vice President of the United States, and six other women—an *Outstanding Mother of the Year* by the National Mother's Day Committee.

The cosmetic and fashion awards she has received from important stores and organizations to celebrate her contributions to beauty could fill a book of their own.

Estée Lauder is a woman of the world who has caught the world's imagination. She is a fascinating person who has created a business empire, and a unique personal universe of respect and affection.